Welcome To EASY AIR FRYER

Whether you are
fanatic, are a casual user, or don't
own an air fryer yet, these dishes are
sure to make you sing the praises of
this handy kitchen appliance.

The recipes in this book are designed
to be easy and delicious while also
using as few ingredients as possible.
That means you'll get all the flavor
you crave without the extra time and
hands-on effort, so you can spend
more time out of the kitchen and with
your family.

Meet
THE AUTHOR

Samantha Lynn is the person
behind the popular website
Everyday Family Cooking.
She has a passion for cooking
and creating simple yet
flavorful air fryer recipes in
the kitchen for her husband
and their two young kids.

Follow her culinary creations
on the blog, Instagram, and
Facebook.

CONTENTS

CONTENTS

CONTENTS

CONTENTS

CONTENTS

CONTENTS

CONTENTS

Must-Have
ACCESSORIES
FOR YOUR AIR FRYER

There are so many air fryer accessories to choose from, it can be hard to know which are best.

Cosori Basket Air Fryer

The number one question I get asked is which air fryer I recommend. I've tried many, and the Cosori basket air fryer is my personal favorite. It has a compact footprint and works great.

Air Fryer Parchment Paper

Using parchment paper will keep your clean-up to a minimum. However, for your air fryer to work correctly, the circulation of air is vital. That's why you'll need specialty parchment paper that is made with holes for airflow.

EVO Oil Mister

To get the best results when air frying, you'll frequently need some sort of oil to spritz your food with oil. The EVO Oil Sprayer consistently does the job without getting gunked up like most other brands.

Instant-Read Thermometer

Using an instant-read thermometer means you'll never second guess whether your meat is cooked through again.

Air Fryer TIPS AND TRICKS

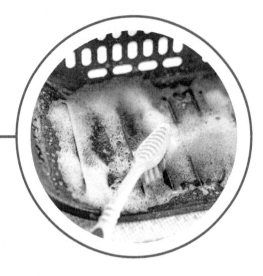

CLEAN AFTER EVERY USE

Your air fryer needs to be cleaned after every use. To do so, remove the basket and drawer and fill them with hot water and degreasing dish soap. Let sit for 10-15 minutes, then use a non- abrasive sponge to gently remove any sticky grease. Deep clean your air fryer every month by spraying it with Dawn Powerwash Spray (spot test first). Let it sit for 10-15 minutes, then use a toothbrush to scrub. Rinse and dry.

DON'T OVERFILL

You should never overcrowd your fryer. Most manuals will say not to fill more than halfway, but I don't even get close to that. If you do, it will obstruct the airflow and you will not get even heat. I get best results when everything is on a single layer. If you need to, it's better to cook in batches so you can still get the crispiness you are expecting.

STOP THE SMOKE

Excess grease, burning food, too much sauce, or an overcrowded basket can make your air fryer smoke. A good method to use when cooking greasy food is to place one or two slices of bread under the basket. Another effective way to stop your air fryer from smoking is to pour two tablespoons of water underneath the basket before you begin cooking. You can also do this to put an end to smoke that appears in the middle of cooking as well.

DELICIOUS
Air Fryer
BREAKFASTS

Crispy BACON

READY IN 8 MIN   **SERVES 4**

You'll never use a griddle again after you try this air fryer bacon recipe.
This super quick method will have you serving up the crispiest bacon in
less than 10 minutes thanks to your air fryer!

DIRECTIONS

Preheat your air fryer to 350 degrees.

Place 1-2 pieces of bread at the bottom of your air fryer
underneath the basket. This will catch any grease and will
help prevent your air fryer from smoking.

Then place the bacon in the air fryer evenly in one layer. Cut
the bacon in half if it's too long.

Cook in the air fryer for 8-10 minutes until it's at your desired
crispiness. Remove with tongs and place bacon on a plate
lined paper towels to remove excess grease, then enjoy!

TIPS

Want extra-crispy bacon or need to fry up some bacon bits?
Cook your bacon for an additional 1-2 minutes.

INGREDIENTS

7 ounces of bacon
(approximately 8 slices)

Optional

1-2 pieces of bread (to
prevent smoking)

Breakfast SAUSAGE

READY IN **7 MIN**   SERVES **1-7**

INGREDIENTS

2 to 14 breakfast sausage links, raw and refrigerated

DIRECTIONS

Preheat your air fryer to 380 degrees.

Carefully place the sausage in the air fryer in rows, leaving room between them for the air to circulate.

Cook for 7-9 minutes. Depending on how done you like your sausage, you can add 1 more minute. The internal temperature should be 160, and there should be no more pink color in the sausage.

TO MAKE SAUSAGE PATTIES

Prefer patties? No problem! To make sausage patties in the air fryer, preheat your machine to 370 degrees. Then place the raw sausage patties (I usually do 8) in the air fryer in a single layer, with space in between each. Remember, it's better to cook in batches than to overcrowd the basket!

Cook for 6-8 minutes until the sausage reaches an internal temperature of 160 degrees. Then remove from the air fryer and enjoy.

Perfect TOAST

INGREDIENTS

4 slices of the
bread of your
choice (I used
white bread)

Toppings of your
choice (see the next
page for toast
topping ideas)

DIRECTIONS

Preheat your air fryer to 400 degrees F.

Place your slices of bread in the basket.

Cook for 2 minutes and then flip and cook for
1 more minute.

Spread your toppings and enjoy.

NOTE

If you find the bread moving around in the
basket, place a wired rack on top of the
bread while it cooks.

TIPS

If you're working with thinner bread or an
extra-thick slice, you may want to adjust the
cooking time. Try subtracting or adding a
minute to start and experimenting from there
until you find the ideal cook time.

The *Best* TOPPINGS FOR TOAST

PLAIN JANE

Toast is one of those foods that often remind me the simplest things in life are the best. There's nothing like sinking your teeth into a piece of bread that's crisp on the outside and soft inside. I typically dress my plain toast with a bit of butter and enjoy it on its own or alongside some of my favorite breakfast foods. Bonus: This also happens to be how my kids enjoy toast best too!

SAVORY STYLE

In the mood for a hearty breakfast? Load up your toast with protein-packed foods such as eggs, sausage, or bacon. I particularly enjoy whipping up a fried egg with a runny yolk and dipping my toast into it. Or, I'll opt for scrambled eggs and layer on some avocado slices with a sprinkle of feta cheese to enjoy.

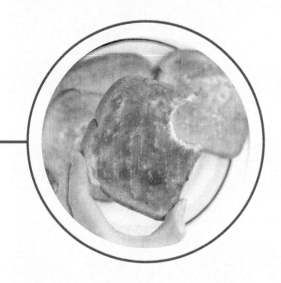

SWEETEN THE DEAL

I'll admit it. From time to time, I have a sweet tooth. On those mornings when I crave something sweet, I'll top my toast with cream cheese and jam, a smear of peanut butter (with or without jelly), or even some Nutella if I feel extra indulgent. Want to scratch that sugar itch but keep it on the healthier side? Enjoy your toast with some fresh berries and a bit of powdered sugar.

Potato PANCAKES

READY IN **19 MIN**   SERVES **4-6**

INGREDIENTS

3 cups of shredded
hash browns

salt and pepper to
taste

1 tsp of garlic

1 tsp of paprika

¼ cup of all
purpose flour

1 egg

2-3 green onions

DIRECTIONS

Combine your shredded hash browns, garlic,
paprika, salt and pepper, flour, and egg in a
large bowl.

Chop your green onions, the green part only,
and incorporate them into the mixture.

Preheat your air fryer to 370 degrees. While
it is preheating, make your pancakes. I took a
¼ cup measuring cup and scooped the
mixture into it. I then shook it out and it was
formed like the measuring cup. I simply
pressed down on the mixture to make it into
the pancake form.

Once your air fryer is ready, generously spray
the bottom of your basket. Lay your potato
cakes in the basket. Do not overcrowd it
because you will need room to flip them
halfway through the cooking time.

Cook for 4 minutes and then flip. Spray the
tops of your potato pancakes and cook for an
additional 4-5 minutes.

Serve with a dollop of sour cream and
additional green onions, if desired.

Crispy HASHBROWNS

READY IN **25 MIN**   SERVES **4**

DIRECTIONS

Preheat your air fryer to 370 degrees F.

Spread the frozen hash browns in a single layer inside, spray the top of the hash brown layer with olive oil spray, then sprinkle with garlic powder, salt, and pepper to taste.

Cook for 18 minutes. Then, use a spatula to divide the hash browns and carefully flip them. Spray with olive oil spray and continue to air fry for about 5 more minutes, or until they're golden brown and crispy to your liking.

Remove to a serving plate, season with additional salt and pepper if desired, and serve.

TIPS

The secret to getting crispy hashbrowns in the air fryer is to use frozen hashbrowns rather than fresh. The freezing process helps release moisture from the potato, resulting in a crispier finish. It's also important not to overcrowd the fryer —it's better to cook in smaller batches than a large one.

INGREDIENTS

16 oz frozen shredded hash brown potatoes

½ tsp garlic powder

Kosher salt, to taste

Black pepper, to taste

Olive oil spray

Crispy
BREAKFAST POTATOES

READY IN **40 MIN**   SERVES **4**

INGREDIENTS

1 ½ pounds of small potatoes

2 cups cold water

1 tbsp fresh thyme or 1 tsp dried thyme

½ tbsp minced garlic

½ tbsp olive oil

Juice of ½ a lemon, about 2 tbsps of a medium size lemon

Salt to taste

Looking for the best way to serve potatoes with minimal prep? Air fryer diced breakfast potatoes are crispy, fluffy, and so simple to make!

DIRECTIONS

Wash your potatoes and dice them into small cubes of the same size.

Soak the cut potatoes for 10 minutes in cold water. Once they have soaked, drain them and then pat them dry with a paper towel.

Combine potatoes with thyme, garlic, olive oil, and lemon juice.

Place diced potatoes in your air fryer basket. Cook at 380 degrees F for 20 to 25 minutes, giving the basket a good shake at the 10-minute mark.

Sprinkle more fresh thyme to the potatoes before serving or some zest from your lemon, or both!

TIPS

Want the crispiest potatoes possible? These 3 tips will help!

Firstly, the closer the diced potato pieces are in size, the more evenly they will cook.

Secondly, make sure to soak the diced potatoes in cold water. This will help remove some starch and allow them to crisp up more.

Lastly, make sure to cook the potatoes in a single layer in the air fryer and shake the basket at the halfway mark so the pieces can crisp up on all sides.

Silky SCRAMBLED EGGS

READY IN **12 MIN**   SERVES **2**

Make scrambled eggs the star of the show with this rich, buttery recipe
that comes together in about ten minutes. Once you try this air fryer
method, you'll never go back to the stovetop version again!

DIRECTIONS

Place butter in an oven/air fryer-safe pan and place it
inside the air fryer.

Cook at 300 degrees until butter is melted, about 2
minutes.

Whisk together the eggs and milk, then add salt and
pepper to taste.

Place eggs in the pan and cook them at 300 degrees
for 3 minutes, then push eggs to the inside of the pan
to stir them around.

Cook for 2 more minutes, then add cheddar cheese,
stirring the eggs again.

Cook once more for 2 more minutes. Remove pan from
the air fryer and enjoy them immediately.

INGREDIENTS

⅓ tbsp unsalted butter

2 eggs

2 tbsp milk

salt and pepper to taste

⅛ cup cheddar cheese

Creamy HARD BOILED EGGS

READY IN **20 MIN**   SERVES **4**

An easy and fast alternative to boiling eggs on your stovetop, these air
fryer hard boiled eggs are cooked to perfection every time!

DIRECTIONS

Preheat the air fryer to 270 degrees F.

Place eggs in the air fryer, preferably on a wire rack,
and cook for 15-17 minutes.

Immediately place eggs in a bowl full of cold water and
ice until cool, at least 5 minutes.

Peel eggs and top with salt and pepper, or refrigerate
for up to one week.

TIPS

Cook for slightly longer if you want a stiffer yolk and a
little less for jammy eggs or even soft boiled eggs.

INGREDIENTS

4 eggs*

salt and pepper to taste

*Use slightly older eggs for
easy peeling. I like to use
mine when they're set to
expire in a week to use
them all up.

Perfect FRIED EGGS

READY IN **5 MIN**   SERVES **2**

INGREDIENTS

2 large eggs   Salt and pepper to
                      taste

DIRECTIONS

Spray the insides of 2 small (3- to 4-inch)
cake or pie pans with non-stick cooking
spray, then place them in the basket of an air
fryer.

Preheat the air fryer at 350 degrees. Crack
an egg into each pan and carefully close the
air fryer.

Cook for 3 minutes until most of the white is
set. Lower the heat to 300 degrees F and
cook for 1 to 2 minutes until the whites are set
but the yolks are still runny.

Season with salt and pepper and serve while
warm. I like to enjoy these with toast and
bacon!

TIPS

If you're worried about the yolks breaking, try
cracking your eggs into a small bowl first and
then pouring them into the cake or pie pan.

Additionally, make sure to spray the cake or
pie pans so the eggs will slide out easily right
onto your plate once cooked.

Grab-And-Go EGG CUPS

READY IN 25 MIN   **SERVES 8**

INGREDIENTS

4 large eggs

3 tbsp heavy cream

½ cup cheddar, shredded

4 Bella mushrooms, diced

1 cup fresh spinach, chopped

½ red bell pepper, diced

½ tsp garlic powder

½ tsp onion powder

½ tsp dried oregano

½ tsp salt

½ tsp freshly ground pepper

DIRECTIONS

Whisk together the eggs and heavy cream.

Add the cheddar, mushrooms, spinach, bell pepper, garlic and onion powder, oregano, salt and pepper. Stir well.

Divide the mixture between 8 silicone muffin cups.

Set the air fryer to 400 F and bake for 13-15 minutes.

TIPS

Swap out (or add to!) the ingredients to create custom creations. Pre-cooked sausage or bacon crumbles are an easy addition that my kids love!

Veggie
FRITTATA

READY IN **30 MIN**   SERVES **2**

INGREDIENTS

Small bunch of green onions

1 sweet pepper (whichever your favorite is)

1 medium tomato

½ cup shredded spinach

Handful of champignons (or other mushroom)

4 eggs

2 egg whites (optional, but it makes the frittata more tender)

½ cup Greek yogurt

1 tbsp extra virgin olive oil

½ cup grated parmesan cheese

Salt and pepper to taste

Want to enjoy a breakfast that is filling yet healthy? Look no further than this delicious, easy veggie frittata. This dish is absolutely packed with both vegetables and protein, along with plenty of flavor that the whole family can enjoy.

DIRECTIONS

Preheat the air fryer to 350 degrees.

Meanwhile, chop the green onions, pepper, tomato, spinach, and mushrooms.

Find a small air fryer pan or cake pan that will fit in your air fryer basket. Then spray the bottom with oil or line it with parchment paper. Next, place the chopped veggies on the bottom.

Lightly beat the eggs with the egg whites and Greek yogurt, add the oil and cheese and stir together. Add salt and pepper. Pour the mixture over the veggies.

Bake at 350 degrees F for about 20 minutes.

Serve the frittata hot garnished with fresh green onions.

Breakfast
BURRITOS

READY IN **35 MIN**   SERVES **6**

INGREDIENTS

1 medium potato

1 tbsp oil

1 tsp salt, and more to taste

½ tsp pepper, and more to taste

½ lb raw breakfast sausage

4 eggs

¼ cup milk, preferably whole milk

1 cup shredded cheddar cheese

6 flour tortillas

These tasty air fryer breakfast burritos with egg, sausage, potato, and cheese are ready in about 35 minutes! They can also be frozen for easy future breakfasts.

DIRECTIONS

Preheat your air fryer to 400 degrees.

Chop your potatoes into 1/2-inch cubes and coat them with oil, salt, and pepper. Place them in the air fryer and cook the potatoes for about 8 minutes, then remove and set aside.

Meanwhile, brown the sausage in a skillet on medium heat, breaking them into crumbles until cooked. Remove from the skillet and set aside, keeping the grease in the pan.

Whisk the eggs, milk, and a little salt and pepper to taste in a bowl and add it hot skillet with the sausage grease. Scramble the eggs until they turn fluffy. Remove from the skillet and set aside.

Combine the cooked potatoes, cooked sausage, scrambled eggs, and cheddar cheese in a bowl, then add the mix evenly into the 6 tortillas and wrap them closed. You can use a toothpick to keep them closed.

Spray the burritos with an oil mister and place them into the air fryer. Cook at 380 degrees for 7 to 8 minutes, spraying the burrito and flipping it about halfway through cooking.

Remove the breakfast burritos from the air fryer and enjoy!

TIPS

These breakfast burritos can be frozen for up to 3 months by wrapping them tightly in foil, then in a plastic freezer bag before placing them in the freezer. To reheat from frozen, preheat your air fryer to 370 degrees, and cook for 10-11 minutes. Spray with oil when halfway through cooking.

Chewy
BAGELS

READY IN **35 MIN**   SERVES **4**

INGREDIENTS

1 ½ cups flour

1 tbsp sugar

Pinch of salt

⅓ tsp active dry yeast

1 cup Greek yogurt

1 egg

1 tbsp extra virgin olive oil

Your choice of toppings
(see Tips section for ideas)

Enjoy fresh bagels as part of your weekend brunch with this simple recipe. The air fryer gives them a slightly crispy exterior and a perfect chewy interior that your teeth will sink right into.

DIRECTIONS

Preheat the air fryer to 400 degrees F.

In a large mixing bowl combine flour, sugar, salt and dry yeast, whisk to combine.

Add yogurt, egg, and olive oil, and stir to combine everything. If the dough becomes too sticky, add a little more flour.

Next, separate dough into equal sized balls. Shape them into bagels. You can use whatever method you find easiest, but I typically make a ball, stretch it out a bit and then put a hole in the center.

Spray the surface of your air fryer basket with oil, or line basket with a piece of air fryer parchment paper.

Arrange bagels on the basket surface, then brush with beaten egg and add your favorite topping (see Tips section below for more ideas.)

Bake bagels at 300 degrees F for 20-25 minutes, until golden brown and baked through.

TIPS

One of my favorite things about homemade bagels is that there are so many fun flavor combinations to try. Some of my family's favorite things to add to our bagels include asiago cheese, everything but the bagel seasoning, sesame seeds and sea salt, poppy seeds, and even blueberries!

Fluffy PANCAKES

READY IN 41 MIN　　　　**SERVES 5-6**

INGREDIENTS

1 ½ cups all-purpose flour

1 ½ tsp baking powder

2-3 tsp granulated sugar

¼ tsp kosher salt

1 large egg

1 ½ cups buttermilk (or regular milk)

2 tbsp unsalted butter, melted and slightly cooled

These fool-proof buttermilk hotcakes cook inside a 6-inch cake pan for fluffy, golden pancakes every time. You don't even have to flip them! Oh, and did I mention there are only six ingredients in the homemade batter?

DIRECTIONS

In a mixing bowl, combine flour, baking powder, sugar, and salt. Whisk to combine, then create a well in the center of the dry ingredients.

In a separate bowl, beat the egg, whisk in the milk, then pour in the melted butter. Combine, then pour into the well of the dry ingredients. Gently stir the mixture until just combined, leaving behind a few lumps.

Allow the batter to rest for 5 minutes. Meanwhile, place a 6-inch cake pan inside the basket of your air fryer, close it, and preheat it to 360 degrees F.

Open the air fryer and spray the cake pan with a generous amount of cooking spray. Use an ice cream scoop to drop ½ cup of batter into the cake pan and use a rubber spatula to gently spread the batter to the edges of the pan.

Air fry for 6 to 8 minutes until pancakes are golden brown on top, no need to flip! Repeat with the remaining batter, keeping the cooked pancakes on a baking sheet in an oven set to 200 degrees F until ready to serve.

TIPS

Add chocolate chips, sliced bananas, small berries, or even sprinkles to the batter before air frying for pancakes that are bursting with flavor and fun!

Hearty BAKED OATS

READY IN **25 MIN**   SERVES **2**

DIRECTIONS

Preheat the air fryer to 350 degrees F. Meanwhile, prepare 2 5" ramekins or baking dishes by spraying them with oil.

In a mixing bowl, combine oats and milk and let it sit for 5 minutes. Then, add the butter, egg, sugar, flour, cinnamon, and vanilla. Mix lightly, then carefully fold in the berries.

Spoon the oat mixture into the ramekins. Bake for 15 minutes, until baked through.

TIPS

This is a fun recipe to experiment with, especially for young helpers in the kitchen. Add in different mix-ins to see what your version of the ultimate baked oatmeal muffin is. A few of our favorites include different fruits and berries, nuts, raisins, and seeds.

INGREDIENTS

1 cup oats

½ cup milk

1 tbsp butter, unsalted and melted

1 egg

3 tbsp brown sugar

1 tbsp flour

Vanilla extract

Pinch of cinnamon (optional)

1 cup of berries such as blueberries and/or raspberries

Gooey CINNAMON ROLLS

READY IN 4 MIN   **SERVES 8**

INGREDIENTS

1 can of Pillsbury cinnamon rolls, 8 count (not the Grands)

DIRECTIONS

Preheat your air fryer to 350 degrees.

Place parchment paper in the air fryer (recommended) and carefully place the cinnamon rolls on top, leaving room between each.

Cook the cinnamon rolls for about 4 minutes.

Carefully remove the rolls from your air fryer and allow them to cool for a few minutes, then drizzle icing on top. Enjoy!

TIPS

Cinnamon rolls are best enjoyed warm. If you happen to have leftovers, use the air fryer to reheat them before enjoying them. Just preheat your air fryer to 300 degrees, then cook the cinnamon rolls for a minute.

If you are reheating iced cinnamon rolls, I recommend parchment paper or an air fryer pan for easy clean-up.

Apple
FRITTERS

READY IN **21 MIN**   SERVES **12**

INGREDIENTS

2 apples, cored and diced

1 cup all-purpose flour

2 tbsp sugar

1 tsp baking powder

½ tsp salt

½ tsp ground cinnamon

¼ tsp ground nutmeg

⅓ cup milk

2 tbsp butter, melted (see note)

1 egg

½ tsp lemon juice

Cinnamon Glaze

½ cup confectioners sugar

2 tbsp milk

½ tsp ground cinnamon

Pinch of salt

These apple fritters are air fried and topped with a cinnamon glaze for a delicious breakfast or dessert!

DIRECTIONS

Dice the apples into small cubes and set aside. Peel them if desired.

Add the flour, sugar, baking powder, salt, ground cinnamon, and ground nutmeg into a large mixing bowl and stir to combine. In a separate bowl, mix the milk, butter (see note below), egg, and lemon juice.

Add the wet ingredients to the dry ingredients and stir just until combined. Stir in the apples and put the mixture into the fridge for anywhere from 5 minutes to 2 days (covered).

Preheat your air fryer to 370 degrees.

Put a parchment round on the bottom of the basket and scoop out apple fritters into 2-tablespoon balls. Place apple fritters in the air fryer and cook for 6-7 minutes.

While cooking, whisk the confectioners' sugar, milk, cinnamon, and salt together to make the glaze.

Remove the apple fritters from the air fryer, place them on a wire rack, and immediately pour the glaze over top and enjoy!

NOTE

Want extra fluffy apple fritters? Grate the butter into this recipe cold instead of using melted butter.

Quick FRENCH TOAST

READY IN **15 MIN**   SERVES **5**

DIRECTIONS

Preheat the air fryer to 370 degrees.

Place the eggs, milk, sugar, flour, ground cinnamon, vanilla, and salt into a wide shallow dish.

Whisk to combine. There may be a couple of lumps, but that's okay.

Dip each piece of bread into the egg mixture, making sure to coat on all sides and place into the air fryer in one layer with a parchment round underneath (don't skip this!).

Cook for about 7 to 8 minutes, flipping halfway.

Carefully remove french toast from air fryer and enjoy immediately.

INGREDIENTS

5 slices of bread

2 eggs

⅓ cup milk

3 tbsp sugar

2 tbsp flour

1 tsp ground cinnamon

½ tsp vanilla extract

⅛ tsp salt

Confectioner's sugar for dusting and/or maple syrup for dipping

French TOAST STICKS

READY IN 15 MIN   **SERVES 4**

INGREDIENTS

5 slices of bread

2 eggs

1/3 cup milk

3 tbsp sugar

2 tbsp flour

1 tsp ground cinnamon

1/2 tsp vanilla extract

1/8 tsp salt

Confectioners sugar for dusting (optional)

Maple syrup for dipping (optional)

DIRECTIONS

Preheat your air fryer to 370 degrees.

Cut each piece of bread into 3 equal pieces and set aside.

Put the eggs, milk, sugar, flour, ground cinnamon, vanilla, and salt into a wide shallow dish. Whisk to combine.

Dip each piece of bread into the egg mixture, making sure to coat on all sides.

Place a piece of parchment round paper inside the air fryer and place each french toast stick in one single layer on top of the parchment round (needed to prevent sticking).

Cook for about 10 minutes, flipping halfway through.

Carefully remove the french toast sticks from the air fryer and enjoy immediately, store in the fridge for up to 3 days, or freeze up to 3 months.

Moist BLUEBERRY MUFFINS

READY IN **40 MIN**   SERVES **6**

DIRECTIONS

Preheat the air fryer at 350 degrees F.

Lightly chop the almonds and nuts, and collect the orange zest.

In a mixing bowl, combine the flour, eggs, butter, sugar, milk, vanilla, baking powder, and Greek yogurt (if using). Mix well, preferably with a mixer, so that there are no lumps.

Add the nuts and berries to the batter and mix gently so as not to break the berries.

Fill paper muffin cups ⅔ full. Keep in mind that the dough will rise in the air fryer.

Bake for about 30 minutes until the top is golden. To check readiness, pierce the muffin with a toothpick. If it is wet, then lower the temperature and cook for a few more minutes before checking again.

INGREDIENTS

½ cup walnuts and/or almonds

½ tsp crushed orange zest

⅔ cup all purpose flour

2 eggs

½ cup unsalted butter, softened

½ cup sugar

½ cup milk

1 tsp vanilla

½ tsp baking powder

1 tbsp Greek yogurt (optional)

½ cup blueberries

DELICIOUS
Air Fryer
DINNERS

Classic
HAMBURGER

READY IN 20 MIN   **SERVES 4**

INGREDIENTS

1 pound of ground beef, thawed

1 minced clove of garlic

½ tsp salt

¼ tsp pepper

Buns + your favorite burger toppings for serving

There's nothing I love more than a grilled burger. Except, we live in New York, and it can get down to negative degrees with the windchill here in the winter. That doesn't make good grilling weather. You can imagine my delight when I first tried these air fryer burgers and realized they cooked perfectly. Even better? All the fat drained to the bottom of the fryer, making this recipe just as healthy as on the grill.

DIRECTIONS

Preheat the air fryer to 360 degrees.

Using your hands, mix together the ground beef, garlic, salt, and pepper.

Form into 4 patties. Keep in mind that the higher the fat content, the more your burgers will shrink.

Place patties into the air fryer in a single layer — if you have a smaller air fryer, you may need to cook in batches.

Cook for 8-12 minutes, flipping halfway through cooking for medium-well hamburgers.

TIPS

To make your burgers into cheeseburgers, wait until the burgers are cooked, then turn off the air fryer. Open the door, add the cheese on top, and close the drawer. Allow 1-2 minutes for the cheese to melt. Thicker slices may need additional time.

Simple
MEATBALL PARMESAN SUB

READY IN **12 MIN**   SERVES **2**

If you, like my husband, love Subway's meatball parm sub, then you'll love this copycat recipe! This is also a great option for picky eaters as you can serve the sandwich deconstructed with the meatballs, sauce, bread, and cheese all separately for them to graze on.

INGREDIENTS

8 frozen meatballs

1 cup of marinara sauce (room temperature or warmed)

¼ tsp dried oregano

2 tbsp shredded Parmesan cheese

2 sub or sandwich rolls

DIRECTIONS

Preheat the air fryer to 320 degrees.

Cook the frozen meatballs for 9-11 minutes, shaking halfway through until the internal temperature reaches 160 degrees.

Remove the meatballs from the air fryer and toss in the marinara sauce and oregano.

Add the meatballs to sub rolls and spoon on 2 tablespoons of marinara sauce on top remaining from the bowl.

Top the sub sandwich with freshly grated Parmesan cheese.

Turn the air fryer to 350 degrees, slowly place meatball parm subs inside the air fryer, and cook for 2 minutes until the cheese is melted and the sauce is warmed.

Carefully remove subs from the air fryer, top with more Parmesan cheese if desired, and enjoy!

Moist
MEATLOAF

READY IN **45 MIN**   SERVES **6**

INGREDIENTS

Meatloaf

2 pounds 80/20 ground beef

2 large eggs

¼ cup milk

⅔ cup Italian breadcrumbs

1 packet McCormick's meatloaf seasoning packet (1.5 ounce)

1 tbsp Worcestershire sauce

Topping

1 cup of ketchup

½ cup light brown sugar

1 tbsp dijon mustard

½ tbsp Worchestershire sauce

This air fryer meatloaf gets a wonderful crisp on the outside and turns out perfectly moist without being greasy. This recipe is perfect for feeding the family on busy nights! Serve with mashed potatoes and your choice of green veggie.

DIRECTIONS

Preheat your air fryer to 350 degrees.

Combine the beef, eggs, milk, bread crumbs, meatloaf seasoning, and Worcestershire sauce in a large bowl. You can use a large spoon or just use your hands.

Form the mixture into a loaf shape and place the meatloaf in the air fryer.

Cook it for 25 minutes.*

While the meatloaf is cooking, combine the ketchup, brown sugar, dijon mustard, and Worcestershire sauce in a small bowl.

After 25 minutes, spoon ¼ cup of the topping mixture onto the meatloaf. Place it back in the air fryer and cook for 5 to 10 minutes more until it reaches 165 degrees F.

Remove the meatloaf from the air fryer and top with additional ketchup mixture, and enjoy!

NOTE

*If you are using an air fryer oven, your meatloaf may take longer to come to temperature. Cook it for about 35 minutes, then add the topping on to avoid any burning.

Restaurant-Quality SIRLOIN STEAK

READY IN **50 MIN**   SERVES **2**

INGREDIENTS

2 (8-10 ounce) sirloin steaks, ¾-1 inch thick

Kosher salt and black pepper to taste

4 tbsp butter, softened

1 tbsp fresh parsley, minced

½ tbsp fresh rosemary, minced

1 clove garlic, minced

DIRECTIONS

Allow the steak to sit at room temperature for 30 minutes before cooking.

Preheat your air fryer to 400 degrees F. Season the steak on both sides with a generous pinch of salt and several grinds of black pepper.

Place the steak in the center of the air fryer basket and cook until desired doneness, about 8-10 minutes for medium-rare, 10-12 minutes for medium and 12-15 minutes for medium-well to well-done. Transfer the steak to a cutting board and allow it to rest for about 10 minutes.

Meanwhile, mash together the butter, parsley, chives, garlic, and rosemary in a small bowl until well combined. You can use some crushed red pepper to add some heat if you would like! Slice the steak against the grain into ¼-inch-thick pieces. Top with the garlic-herb butter.

Southern-Style
CHICKEN FRIED STEAK

READY IN **17 MIN**   SERVES **4**

INGREDIENTS

Chicken Fried Steak

1 lb of cube steak, cut into 4 to 6 portions

½ cup all-purpose flour

1 tsp garlic powder

½ tsp paprika

½ tsp salt

¼ tsp pepper

1 large egg

¼ cup water

Gravy

2 tbsp butter

2 tbsp flour

¾ cup milk

salt and pepper to taste

This air fryer chicken fried steak is made with cubed steak to create a crispy and tender weeknight meal. Cover it with the 3-ingredient gravy and serve with your choice of air fryer vegetables for a true southern-style dish.

DIRECTIONS

Preheat your air fryer to 370 degrees.

Remove the cube steaks from the fridge and place them on a cutting board.

In a shallow bowl, combine the flour, garlic powder, paprika, salt, and pepper.

In a second bowl, combine the egg and water and whisk.

Take each portion of the cube steak and dip it into the flour mixture, the egg mixture, then back into the flour mixture, making sure it is fully coated.

Place each piece of chicken fried steak in the air fryer in one layer and cook for 12 to 15, flipping and spraying with oil on both sides halfway through cooking.

Meanwhile, prepare the gravy by melting the butter in a small saucepan on medium heat and slowly whisking in the flour, milk, salt, and pepper. Cook until thickened, then remove from heat. You can add more milk to get the consistency you like.

Remove the chicken fried steak from the air fryer and pour the gravy over top before serving.

Mouth-Watering PRIME RIB STEAK

READY IN **100 MIN**   SERVES **5-6**

DIRECTIONS

Preheat your air fryer to 390 degrees.

Rub the prime rib with olive oil generously, then sprinkle it with salt, black pepper, paprika, and garlic powder.

Cover the prime rib with crushed garlic, then the rosemary and thyme. I recommend using fresh rosemary and thyme for the best flavoring, but you can use dried as well.

Gently place the prime rib in the air fryer and cook for 20 minutes.

Leaving the prime rib steak in the air fryer, turn the temperature down to 315 degrees and continue to cook for about 55 additional minutes until it reaches the desired doneness—about 130 degrees for medium-rare.

Let the prime rib sit for 20 to 30 minutes, then slice and enjoy!

INGREDIENTS

6 pound Prime Rib

3 tbsp olive oil

1 ½ tsp salt

1 ½ tsp black pepper

1 tsp smoked paprika

1 tsp garlic powder

¼ cup minced garlic (about 10 cloves)

One sprig fresh rosemary, chopped (or ½ tsp dried rosemary)

One sprig fresh thyme, chopped (or ½ tsp dried thyme)

INGREDIENTS

Pickling packet that came
with your corned beef*

¼ cup brown mustard

1 tbsp apple cider vinegar

4-pound corned beef
brisket

*if your corned beef didn't
come with a pickling
packet, you can buy it
online or make your own
pickling spice and use a
few teaspoons

Ultra-Tender
CORNED BEEF
READY IN **115 MIN**   SERVES **6-8**

This air fryer corned beef turns out so tender and delicious
that you will find yourself wanting to make this St. Patrick's
Day classic all year round!

DIRECTIONS

Preheat your air fryer to 360 degrees F.

Mix the contents of the pickling packet with the mustard and
apple cider vinegar, forming a paste.

Set the brisket on a large sheet of aluminum foil sprayed
lightly with cooking oil. Brush ⅔ of the mustard paste over
the whole brisket, reserving the rest, then fold the foil
around the brisket.

Place the wrapped brisket in the air fryer basket and cook
for 1 hour.

When the timer goes off, pull back the foil, baste the brisket
with the remaining sauce, and cover. Cook for another 40
minutes.

Pull back the foil and cook for 5 minutes at 400 degrees, if
you'd like a nice top.

TIPS

Thanks to the signature red color, it can be hard to know
when corned beef is fully cooked. It should be cooked to at
least a medium level of doneness, which means you want the
internal temperature to reach 145 degrees F minimum.
However, I prefer mine cooked a bit longer as it becomes
more tender!

Tender STEAK BITES

READY IN 40 MIN   **SERVES 4-6**

INGREDIENTS

2 lb sirloin steak

1 tbsp extra virgin olive oil

1 tbsp melted butter

1 tbsp soy sauce

½ tsp ground black pepper

½ tsp onion powder

½ tsp chili powder

Pinch of kosher salt

Dry oregano and rosemary (to your taste - about ½ to 1 tsp)

DIRECTIONS

Preheat the air fryer to 400 degrees F.

In a mixing bowl, whisk together the olive oil, butter, soy sauce, pepper, onion powder, chili powder, salt, and herbs to make the marinade.

Cut the beef into bite pieces, combine with marinade, and rest for 5-10 minutes.

Arrange the pieces in a single layer in an oiled air fryer basket.

Cook the beef bites in the preheated air fryer for 20-25 minutes, turning once halfway, then reduce the temperature to 270 degrees F and let the bites slowly cook for 5 more minutes.

5-Layer
LASAGNA

READY IN **60 MIN**   SERVES **4**

INGREDIENTS

2 tbsp extra virgin olive oil

1 onion

2 chopped carrots

3 cloves minced garlic

1 - 1.5 lb ground beef

1 14.5 oz can crushed tomatoes (may not use the entire can)

1 tsp Italian seasoning

½ tsp granulated garlic

½ tsp kosher salt

½ tsp black pepper

1 pack lasagna noodles (cooked or no-cook style)

1 cup shredded mozzarella cheese

5 creamy layers filled with ground beef, sauce, cheese, and spices are cooked to perfection with a golden brown outside, then topped with even more cheese. This is what air fryer dreams are made of!

DIRECTIONS

Preheat your air fryer to 350 degrees F.

Heat a large skillet with oil over medium heat. Add onion and carrots and cook for about 5 minutes. Add in the garlic and cook another minute, until fragrant. Then, add the beef and cook until browned. Stir in tomatoes, Italian seasoning, granulated garlic, salt, and black pepper, and allow to simmer for 5 minutes.

In a greased dish that fits in the air fryer, add a layer of lasagna noodles. Spoon on enough of the ground beef mixture to cover the pasta, then top with mozzarella cheese. Keep repeating until your baking dish is filled with layers. I did 5, but you could do more or less.

Sprinkle the top layer well with cheese.

Cover the lasagna with foil, and bake at 350 degrees F for 25-30 minutes. Then, remove the foil and raise the temperature to 400 degrees F. Bake for an additional 10-15 minutes, until golden brown.

Let the dish stand for about 10 minutes before slicing. If desired, garnish with more cheese and some fresh basil before serving.

TIPS

The amount of time needed to cook may vary depending on the size of your lasagna and the size of your air fryer. Use a toothpick or fork to test if the noodles are cooked.

INGREDIENTS

⅓ cup olive oil

2 tbsp soy sauce

2 tbsp brown sugar

Juice of 1 lime

1 4-ounce can green chiles, diced

4 cloves garlic, minced

¼ cup fresh cilantro leaves, chopped

1 tsp kosher salt

1 tsp cumin

1 tsp oregano

½ tsp paprika

½ tsp black pepper

1 pound skirt steak (or flank steak)

Flavorful
CARNE ASADA

READY IN **4 HOURS, 20 MINUTES**   SERVES **4**

After a simple marinade, this flavorful air fryer skirt steak cook ups in about 6 minutes! Enjoy carne asada for a quick and easy weeknight dinner the whole family will love.

DIRECTIONS

In a measuring cup, combine olive oil, soy sauce, brown sugar, lime juice, chiles, garlic, cilantro, salt, cumin, oregano, paprika, and pepper. Place the steak in a gallon-size zipper bag and pour the liquid into the bag. Seal and marinate for at least 4 hours (or overnight), turning the bag at least once.

Remove the steak from the marinade and allow it to come to room temperature for at least 20 to 30 minutes.

Preheat your air fryer to 400 degrees.

Place the skirt steak in the air fryer and cook for 3 minutes. Flip the steak, then cook for an additional 3 minutes (for medium-rare; increase time to 8 minutes total for medium, 10 to 12 for well).

Transfer the steak to a cutting board, tent it with aluminum foil, and allow it to rest for 5 to 10 minutes before serving.

Homemade EMPANADAS

READY IN **26 MIN**   SERVES **6**

INGREDIENTS

1 tbsp olive oil

½ small onion, diced

⅓ bell pepper, finely diced

5 oz ground beef

½ tsp paprika

½ tsp ground cumin

½ tsp dried oregano

½ tsp dried thyme

½ tsp salt

½ tsp freshly ground pepper

¾ package puff pastry dough

1 egg, whisked

Marinara sauce, to serve

DIRECTIONS

Heat the olive oil in a skillet.

Add the onion and sauté for 3-4 minutes. Add the bell pepper and cook for 2 minutes. Bring in the ground beef and stir to break it down. Cook for 5 minutes. Then season with paprika, cumin, oregano, thyme, salt and pepper. Cook for 3-4 minutes more.

Preheat the air fryer to 400 F.

Cut the dough into disks, about 5 ½ inches diameter.

Add 1-2 tablespoons of beef filling in the center of each disk. Fold one disk at a time, pinching edges to seal. Use the tips of a fork to create a pattern on the edges. Brush the empanadas with whisked egg.

Bake for 5-8 minutes, until golden brown on top. Serve with marinara sauce, if desired.

Stuffed
PEPPERS

READY IN **37 MIN**   SERVES **4**

INGREDIENTS

4 bell peppers

1 cup of cooked rice

1 tbsp of olive oil

1 lb of lean ground beef

Salt and pepper to taste

½ onion, chopped

½ tbsp minced garlic

2 cups of tomato sauce

1 tsp of Italian seasoning

¾ cup of shredded
mozzarella

Optional: parsley for
garnish

These tasty air fryer stuffed peppers are so easy to make! The ground beef and rice filling is super satisfying, while the melty cheese on top adds the perfect finishing touch.

DIRECTIONS

Preheat your air fryer to 300 degrees.

Cut the tops of the peppers off and then scrape out the seeds.

Cook your rice according to the package directions.

Brush your peppers with olive oil, inside and out. Place them into the air fryer basket and cook for 5 minutes.

While the peppers are cooking, season your beef with salt and pepper then brown it with the onions and garlic, in a medium saucepan, over medium high heat. Cook till there is no more pink in the beef and then drain the grease.

Add the cooked rice, tomato sauce, and Italian seasoning to your beef mixture and simmer for 4 minutes.

Scoop the beef mixture into the peppers and place them back into the air fryer. Cook at 350 degrees for 8 minutes. Top them with the shredded mozzarella and place back into the air fryer for another 3-4 minutes, till the tops are golden brown.

Remove from the air fryer and enjoy. Top with chopped parsley for additional garnish before serving.

Bone-in CHICKEN THIGHS

READY IN **25 MIN**   SERVES **3**

INGREDIENTS

3 bone-in, skin-on
chicken thighs

½ tsp garlic
powder

Salt and pepper, to
taste

½ tsp onion
powder

2 tsp olive oil

1 tbsp poultry
seasoning

DIRECTIONS

Preheat your air fryer to 380 degrees F.

Season your chicken thighs with salt and
pepper. Drizzle the olive oil over the thighs.

Combine the garlic powder, onion powder,
and poultry seasoning in a small bowl. Rub
the seasoning onto your thighs till they are
covered. You may have some remaining
seasoning.

Place your chicken thighs in the air fryer
basket and cook for 12 minutes, and then flip
them. Continue to cook for an additional 6 to
7 minutes or until a meat thermometer reads
an internal temperature of 165 degrees F.

Allow them to rest for a few minutes and
serve.

Optional: Garnish them with fresh parsley.

Crispy
FRIED CHICKEN

READY IN **40 MIN**   SERVES **6-8**

INGREDIENTS

3 pounds bone-in chicken thighs and drumsticks

1 ½ cups buttermilk

2 large eggs

2 cups all-purpose flour

3 tsp paprika

2 tsp garlic powder

2 tsp onion powder

2 tsp salt

1 tsp black pepper

Olive oil spray

This is the stuff air fryer dreams are made of! Crispy, juicy, Southern fried chicken legs are made with buttermilk and have the perfect crunch when you bite into them. Because they are made in the air fryer, this chicken is made without excess grease and oil. Hands down, this is the best way to enjoy fried chicken at home.

DIRECTIONS

Preheat your air fryer to 360 degrees F.

In a large shallow bowl, whisk together the buttermilk and eggs until well combined.

In a second shallow bowl, add the flour, paprika, garlic powder, onion powder, salt, and pepper and whisk well.

Using tongs or your hands, dip each piece of the chicken in the flour, shaking off any excess. Next, dip it in the buttermilk, then roll it in the flour, covering it completely. Set on a baking sheet and set aside. Repeat with the remaining chicken.

Spray all sides of the chicken pieces with olive oil spray, as well as the inner basket of the air fryer.

Place 4-5 pieces of chicken in the bottom of the air fryer basket, or as many that fit in your air fryer basket or oven in a single layer.

Cook for 15-20 minutes. Carefully flip the chicken and cook for another 5-10 minutes until 165 degrees internally.

Juicy CHICKEN FAJITAS

READY IN **20 MIN**   SERVES **2**

DIRECTIONS

Preheat your air fryer to 370 degrees.

Put the chicken strips, bell pepper, onion, corn oil, chili powder, lime juice, cumin, salt and pepper, and cayenne pepper (if using) in a bowl and mix.

Place the chicken fajitas in the air fryer and cook for 10-13 minutes, shaking the basket halfway through. The fajitas are done when the chicken hits 165 degrees F at its thickest point.

Remove the fajitas from the air fryer and enjoy!

TIPS

I love these fajitas because there are so many different ways you can enjoy them. You can scoop them into warmed tortillas, place on a bed of lettuce, or use your air fryer to make your own homemade tortilla chips and turn this recipe into a delicious plate of nachos.

INGREDIENTS

½ lb boneless, skinless chicken breasts, cut into ½-inch wide strips

1 large red or yellow bell pepper, cut into strips

1 medium red onion, cut into strips

1 tbsp corn oil

1 tbsp chili powder

2 tsp lime juice

1 tsp cumin

Salt and pepper to taste

Pinch of cayenne pepper (optional)

INGREDIENTS

1 pound boneless skinless chicken breasts or chicken thighs

2 tbsp cornstarch or potato starch

Orange Sauce

½ cup orange juice

2 tbsp brown sugar

1 tbsp soy sauce

1 tbsp rice wine vinegar

¼ tsp ground ginger (or ½ tsp freshly grated ginger)

dash of red pepper flakes

zest of one orange

2 tsp cornstarch mixed with 2 tsp water

Optional to Serve

green onions, chopped

sesame seeds

Perfect
ORANGE CHICKEN

READY IN **20 MIN**   SERVES **2**

By using the air fryer in this recipe, you'll get perfect bites of crispy, tangy chicken that rivals your favorite take-out spot.

DIRECTIONS

Preheat the air fryer to 400 degrees.

Combine chicken pieces and cornstarch into a bowl and mix until chicken is just fully coated (see notes above about not overcoating them).

Cook chicken for 7-9 minutes, shaking the basket halfway through or until chicken is just at or above 165 degrees internally.

Meanwhile, combine the orange juice, brown sugar, rice wine vinegar, soy sauce, ginger, red pepper flakes, and orange zest in a small saucepan on medium heat.

Bring mixture to a simmer and simmer for 5 minutes.

Mix cornstarch and water together in a small bowl and add it to the orange sauce.

Let simmer for one additional minute while stirring, then immediately remove from heat.

Remove chicken from the air fryer and combine with sauce.

Top with green onions and sesame seeds if desired, and enjoy immediately!

TIPS

This orange sauce recipe will make just enough sauce to coat the chicken. If you would like extra sauce for a full stir fry, you can double the recipe.

Mess-Free BUFFALO CHICKEN TENDERS

READY IN 25 MIN   **SERVES 2-3**

The buffalo sauce is cooked right into these tenders, so your breading can stay crispy (and mess-free).

INGREDIENTS

1 lb chicken tenders

1 tsp kosher salt

½ tsp black pepper

1 large egg, beaten

¼ cup <u>buffalo sauce</u>, plus more for dipping

1 cup panko bread crumbs

1 tsp paprika

1 tsp garlic powder

Olive oil spray

Ranch or blue cheese dressing, for serving

DIRECTIONS

Preheat the air fryer to 400 degrees F.

Pat chicken tenders dry with paper towels, then season with salt and pepper.

Place egg and buffalo sauce in a shallow bowl and whisk well. In a second shallow bowl, combine the bread crumbs, paprika, and garlic powder.

Dip chicken in the egg mixture, then into the breadcrumb mixture. Shake off excess and place on a large plate. Spray both sides of the chicken generously with oil.

Air fry the chicken tenders for 10-12 minutes, flipping once halfway through the cooking time until they are cooked through and golden brown on the outside.

Serve with more buffalo sauce and your favorite dipping sauce, if desired.

INGREDIENTS

3 boneless, skinless
chicken breasts

salt and pepper to taste

4 oz of cream cheese,
softened

1 ½ cup of chopped
spinach

½ cup of mozzarella

¼ cup of parmesan

3 tbsp diced roasted red
pepper

2 tbsp of mayo

1 ½ tsp minced garlic (1 to
2 cloves)

1 ½ tsp paprika

1 ½ tsp garlic powder

1 ½ tsp onion powder

Stuffed
CHICKEN BREASTS
READY IN **30 MIN**   SERVES **3**

This air fryer stuffed chicken breast is elegant enough to
make for guests while also being easy enough to whip up for
a quick weeknight dinner!

DIRECTIONS

Season your chicken with salt and pepper to taste.

Combine your filling: cream cheese, spinach, parmesan,
roasted red peppers, mayo, and garlic.

Combine your seasonings: paprika, garlic powder, and onion
powder.

Filet your chicken breast lengthwise, without cutting all the
way through. Lay your chicken breast open and season with
½ to 1 teaspoon of the seasoning. Then spread about ½ cup
of the spinach and cheese mixture on one side. Fold your
chicken breast over and then piece toothpicks along the
seam to try and keep as much spinach and cheese inside as it
cooks. Sprinkle the top of your chicken with additional
seasoning.

Brush olive oil in your air fryer basket, as the nonstick spray is
shown to cause your basket to wear faster. Preheat your air
fryer at 380 degrees F.

Lay two breasts in at a time, cooking in batches if you cannot
fit all 3. Cook for 15 to 18 minutes till a meat thermometer
reads 165 degrees F.

TIPS

The most important part of stuffing a chicken breast is
butterflying the meat. This means laying a raw chicken breast
flat, then cutting horizontally through the long end of the
chicken. Make sure you don't slice it all the way through!

Homemade CHICKEN NUGGETS

A family favorite, these air fryer chicken nuggets are tender, crispy, and juicy! These nuggets are the perfect thing to make for a quick dinner or potluck appetizer.

Plus, you'll be amazed at how simple these are to make. It's even easier than going to the grocery store or going through the drive-through at your favorite fast food restaurant.

READY IN **25 MIN**   MAKES **20-25 NUGGETS**

DIRECTIONS

Trim any visible fat off of the edges of your chicken breast. Then cut it into ½-inch strips and then cut those into desired size chunks. (Cut it in half if it is a smaller strip or into thirds for the larger ones.)

Season the chicken with salt and pepper. Allow your chicken to come to room temperature so that when you dip it in the butter, the butter doesn't solidify.

Combine the breadcrumbs, garlic powder, and Italian seasoning and set aside.

Melt your butter in a microwave-safe bowl. Dip your chicken nuggets in the butter first and then in your breadcrumbs.

Preheat the air fryer to 390 degrees F. Place your nuggets in the basket. There is no need to spray your basket since you have used butter to coat your chicken.

Cook for 10 to 12 minutes, flipping halfway through and checking on it the last few minutes since timing will vary on different fryers.

INGREDIENTS

1 large chicken breast, cut into chunks

Salt and pepper to taste

¾ cup Italian breadcrumbs

½ tsp garlic powder

½ tsp Italian seasoning

½ cup melted butter

Juicy
CHICKEN LEGS
READY IN **20 MIN**   SERVES **4**

INGREDIENTS

2 tsp paprika

1 tsp salt

1 tsp oregano

½ tsp garlic powder

½ tsp onion powder

½ tsp brown sugar

¼ tsp black pepper

2 lbs chicken drumsticks

1 tsp olive oil

These air fryer chicken legs are crispy and juicy, and take just 20 minutes to prep and cook! Even better? All you need is some chicken and a variety of seasonings.

DIRECTIONS

Preheat your air fryer to 400F

In a small bowl, stir together the paprika, salt, oregano, garlic powder, onion powder, brown sugar, and black pepper to make the seasoning

Add chicken drumsticks to a large bowl, drizzle with olive oil, sprinkle with seasoning, and toss to coat

Place chicken drumsticks in a single layer in the preheated air fryer basket

Air fry for 15 minutes, flipping halfway through, or until cooked to 165 F.

Serve immediately.

TIPS

For meat that is crisp on the outside and juicy on the inside, it's important to cook your chicken legs in a single layer. If needed, cook your air fryer drumsticks in two batches. It's better to take the extra time since they won't cook properly if you crowd them.

Garlic Chili CHICKEN WINGS

READY IN **30 MIN**   SERVES **2**

DIRECTIONS

Prepare wings by separating the drums and flats and discarding the tips. Then, pat them dry.

In a small mixing bowl, mix the olive oil, honey, garlic, garlic powder, chili powder, paprika, salt, and pepper to make the marinade.

Toss the wings and marinade together and let them sit for a few minutes while you preheat your air fryer to 380 degrees.

Put the wings into the air fryer in one layer with some space between each piece of meat.

Cook the wings for 20-25 minutes until golden brown. Serve immediately and enjoy while warm.

INGREDIENTS

2 lb chicken wings – flats and drumsticks separated and tips discarded

1 tbsp avocado or olive oil

1 tbsp honey

1 garlic clove minced

1 tsp garlic powder

½ tsp chili powder

½ tsp paprika

½ tsp kosher salt

½ tsp ground black pepper

INGREDIENTS

2 boneless, skinless
chicken breasts

2 tbsp sour cream

1 tsp Dijon mustard

1 tsp smoked paprika

1 tsp onion powder

1 tsp Herbs de Provence

½ tsp garlic powder

Juice of ½ lemon

Salt and pepper to taste

For the Salad

1 cup arugula

1 diced tomato

2 oz feta cheese

1 tbsp olive oil

Salt to taste

Additional sour cream for
serving

Marinated
CHICKEN BREASTS
READY IN **60 MIN**   SERVES **2**

This moist marinated chicken breast is bursting with flavor in
every bite. Paired with a simple salad, this is the perfect
light, healthy dinner.

DIRECTIONS

Place the chicken breasts in a large mixing bowl and stir in
the sour cream, dijon mustard, smoked paprika, onion
powder, herbs de Provence, garlic powder, lemon juice,
and salt and pepper.

Mix until the chicken is fully coated with the marinade, and
let it sit for about 30 minutes.

Place the chicken breasts in the air fryer basket. Cook in the
air fryer at 350 F for about 25 minutes.

Meanwhile, prepare the salad. Place the arugula, diced
tomato, and feta cheese on a serving plate, and season with
some salt.

Drizzle with some oil and serve it with the cooked chicken.
Add an additional spoonful of sour cream if you'd like.

TIPS

To make sure your chicken breast is fully cooked, use a meat
thermometer. The internal temperature should be at least
165 degrees.

Flavorful CHICKEN + VEGGIES

READY IN **15 MIN**   SERVES **2-3**

Tired of basic vegetables? This 15-minute chicken and veggie dinner is seasoned then cooked to perfection.

DIRECTIONS

Preheat the air fryer at 400F.

Combine the chicken, veggies, spices, herbs and olive oil and mix well, to coat.

Transfer to the air fryer basket and cook for 15 minutes, stirring once.

Top with fresh parsley and serve.

TIPS

Experiment and see what your favorite vegetable combination is. You may need to adjust the cooking time, but this seasoning mix works well with practically any veggie!

INGREDIENTS

1 large chicken breast, cut into small chunks

½ zucchini, cubed

½ eggplant, cubed

1 red onion, roughly chopped
8 cherry tomatoes

½ tsp garlic powder

½ tsp dried oregano

½ tsp dried basil

1 tsp salt

1 tsp freshly ground pepper

1 tbsp olive oil

2 tbsp fresh parsley, chopped

Seasoned
WHOLE CHICKEN

READY IN **40 MIN**   SERVES **6-8**

INGREDIENTS

4.5 - 5 lb whole raw
chicken

1 tbsp black pepper

1 tbsp onion powder

1 tbsp garlic powder

1 tsp paprika

A whole chicken is roasted in the air fryer with a simple
seasoning made with just 5 ingredients. Serve this with your
favorite sides—I recommend air fryer green beans and some
easy homemade garlic bread.

DIRECTIONS

Preheat your air fryer to 360 degrees.

Remove the neck and giblets from the chicken cavity. Pat
the chicken dry.

Mix the black pepper, onion powder, garlic powder, and
paprika in a bowl, then rub it all over the chicken.

Place the whole chicken into the air fryer breast side down
and cook for 40 minutes*.

Flip the chicken and cook breast side up for another 15 to 20
minutes. The chicken is done when it hits 165 degrees F at its
thickest point.

Remove the chicken from the air fryer, let sit for 5 minutes,
then serve!

NOTE

*Place 1 to 2 slices of bread OR ¼ cup water under the
basket inside the drawer of the air fryer to avoid the air fryer
from smoking.

Marinated PORK TENDERLOIN

READY IN **57 MIN**   SERVES **2**

DIRECTIONS

Remove the pork tenderloin from packaging and set aside.

Mix the olive oil, soy sauce, garlic, brown sugar, dijon mustard, and salt and pepper into a bowl then pour into a gallon zip-topped bag.

Add the pork tenderloin to the bag, close it, and cover it with the marinade. Marinate the pork for at least 30 minutes, but up to 5 days while refrigerated.

Preheat the air fryer to 400 degrees.

Remove the pork tenderloin from the bag and place in the air fryer. Cook for 22 to 25 minutes flipping halfway through until it hits 145 degrees internally.

Let the air fryer pork tenderloin rest for at least 5 minutes, slice into medallions, and enjoy!

INGREDIENTS

1 pork tenderloin

½ cup olive oil

3 tbsp soy sauce

2 cloves garlic, minced

2 tbsp brown sugar

1 tbsp dijon mustard

salt and pepper, to taste

Garlic Butter
PORK CHOPS

READY IN **45 MIN**   SERVES **2**

INGREDIENTS

2 bone-in pork chops

1 tbsp extra virgin olive oil

1 tbsp melted butter

1 minced garlic clove

1 tsp brown sugar

½ tsp granulated garlic

½ tsp Italian seasoning
(optional)

½ tsp ground black pepper

Pinch of kosher salt

These pork chops are cooked in a homemade garlic butter sauce and air fried to perfection. Enjoy tender buttery meat with your favorite side dishes such as baked potatoes, broccoli, or bacon Brussels sprouts.

DIRECTIONS

Preheat the air fryer to 400 degrees F.

In a small mixing bowl, combine the olive oil, butter, garlic, brown sugar, granulated garlic, Italian seasoning, pepper, and salt

Drizzle both sides of the chops with the garlic butter.

Arrange the pork chops in an oiled air fryer basket in a single layer.

Cook the chops in the preheated air fryer for 20 minutes, turning once halfway. Then reduce the temperature to 270 degrees F and cook the chops for 10 more minutes, then allow the meat to rest for 5 minutes.

Drizzle with remaining garlic butter, then serve with your favorite veggies and sides.

TIPS

The amount of time needed to cook may vary depending on the size and thickness of your chops and the size of your air fryer. Cook until an internal temperature of 145 degrees F is reached.

Fall-Off-The-Bone
RIBS

READY IN **50 MIN**   SERVES **4**

Ditch the grill or smoker and whip up air fryer baby back ribs! The beautiful crust on the outside and fall-off-the-bone tender meat on the inside are absolutely crave-worthy.

INGREDIENTS

3 lb rack of pork baby back ribs

3 tsp paprika

2 tsp garlic powder

1 tsp salt

½ tsp brown sugar

½ tsp chili powder

¼ tsp black pepper

1 cup BBQ sauce, plus more as desired

DIRECTIONS

Peel the silverskin from the back of the ribs then cut the rack into 2-3 sections that fit into your air fryer basket.

Preheat the air fryer to 380 degrees F.

Meanwhile, in a small bowl, combine paprika, garlic powder, salt, brown sugar, chili powder, and pepper. Season both sides of the ribs with the spice mixture bbq spice rub, covering both sides well.

Place the rib sections in the air fryer basket, meat side down, and air fry for 15 minutes.

Flip the ribs with a pair of tongs and air fry them for an additional 10-12 minutes.

When the timer is up, open the basket and brush the ribs with BBQ sauce - as much or little as you want. Close the air fryer and cook for another 5 minutes.

Remove the ribs and allow them to rest for 5-10 minutes before serving with additional BBQ sauce if desired.

Country-style RIBS

READY IN **30 MIN**   SERVES **4-5**

INGREDIENTS

2 lb country-style
boneless pork ribs

1 ½ tsp smoked
paprika

½ tsp kosher salt

½ tsp black
pepper

½ tsp garlic
powder

¼ tsp onion
powder

¼ tsp cayenne
pepper

1 cup BBQ sauce

DIRECTIONS

Preheat an air fryer to 370 degrees F.
Combine the paprika, salt, pepper, garlic
powder, onion powder, and cayenne in a
small bowl and set aside.

Trim the ribs, if necessary, and spray or rub
them with cooking oil, then sprinkle the ribs
with the seasoning, massaging in it on all
sides.

Place the country-style ribs in the air fryer in
an even layer. Cook for 20 minutes, flipping
once halfway through at the 10-minute mark.

When the timer goes off, brush them with a
thin layer of BBQ sauce, then place them
back in the basket and cook for 5-8 more
minutes.

Serve with additional BBQ sauce.

Pineapple-Glazed
HAM
READY IN **60 MIN**   SERVES **6-8**

INGREDIENTS

13-lb fully cooked ham
(slightly trimmed to fit your
air fryer)

6 tbsp unsalted butter

3 tbsp brown sugar

1 tbsp honey

1 tbsp pineapple juice
(from can)

3 canned pineapple slices

3 maraschino cherries

You're going to fall in love with the pineapple glaze over this homemade air fryer ham! From holiday feasts to Sunday family dinner, you'll want to make this recipe on repeat.

DIRECTIONS

Add the butter, brown sugar, honey, and pineapple juice to a small saucepan set over medium heat. Bring it to a simmer, then remove it from the heat and set it aside.

Lay two large sheets of aluminum foil in the air fryer basket and set the ham in the middle, folding up the sides slightly.

Brush the ham with ⅓ of the glaze. Fold the foil over the ham to cover, then air fry at 320 degrees F for 20 minutes.

Fold the foil back and brush another ⅓ of the glaze on the ham.

Skewer each maraschino cherry on a toothpick. Hold a slice of pineapple on the top of the ham with one hand, and push the toothpick through the hole and into the ham. Cover the ham with the foil and air fry for another 20 minutes.

Fold the foil back, brush the ham with the remaining glaze, and air fry uncovered for an additional 5-8 minutes at 380 degrees F, until the top is browned and the ham reaches 145 degrees F internally. Allow it to rest for at least 10 minutes before serving with the glaze in the bottom of the foil.

Juicy SPARE RIBS

READY IN **50 MIN**   SERVES **2**

DIRECTIONS

Preheat the air fryer to 400 degrees F.

Set aside the spare ribs. Combine all the other ingredients in a small bowl.

Strip membrane from the back of ribs if needed. Then cut the ribs into 4 equal pieces. Rub the spice mixture all over the ribs.

Arrange the ribs in the air fryer basket in a single layer, meat side down.

Cook ribs in the preheated air fryer for 30 minutes, turning once halfway, then reduce the temperature to 270 degrees F and let the ribs cook for another 10-15 minutes.

Cut ribs into pieces, remove onto a serving plate, and allow to rest for a few minutes. Serve with your favorite sauce and enjoy!

INGREDIENTS

2 lb pork ribs

1 tbsp extra virgin olive oil

1 tbsp honey

1 tsp brown sugar

1 tsp smoked paprika

½ tsp chili powder (according to your taste)

½ tsp granulated garlic

½ tsp ground black pepper

¼ tsp Italian seasoning (Optional)

Chili Lime PORK CHOPS

READY IN **35 MIN**   SERVES **4**

DIRECTIONS

Preheat your air fryer to 400 degrees F.

Combine the chili powder, garlic powder, salt, sugar, and lime zest in a bowl. (You can also use 1 ½ tbsp of store-bought chili lime seasoning instead of homemade seasoning. I use Trader Joe's chile lime seasoning).

Spray your pork chops with olive oil cooking spray, and then cover each pork chop completely with the seasoning.

Place them into the air fryer with a little space around them and cook for 20 to 25 minutes.

You may need to cook in batches. If you have varying thicknesses in your pork chops, then use a meat thermometer on your smallest pork chop and set it at 145 degrees F.

Allow pork chops to cool for 5 minutes before slicing and serving. Enjoy!

INGREDIENTS

2 tsp chili powder

1 tsp garlic powder

½ tsp salt

½ tsp sugar

1 lime zested

4 thick-cut pork chops

Cilantro, optional

Lime wedges, optional

Crispy EGGPLANT PARMESAN

READY IN 35 MIN   **SERVES 4**

This air fryer eggplant parm delivers on all the breaded crunch without the deep-frying! Top with marinara and mozzarella for a vegetarian dish that everyone will love.

DIRECTIONS

Cut the eggplant into ¼ inch slices and place in a colander or baking sheet. Sprinkle the eggplant with salt and let sit for at least 15 minutes.

Place the egg in one bowl and mix the breadcrumbs, Parmesan cheese, garlic powder, and basil in a second bowl.

Dip each eggplant slice into the egg then the breadcrumb mixture making sure to fully coat each slice.

Place each eggplant breaded slice into an air fryer preheated to 370 degrees. Lay pieces in one single layer without pieces touching. Cook for 8 to 10 minutes, spritzing with oil and flipping over halfway.

Put a teaspoon of marinara sauce on top of each eggplant slice and top them with mozzarella cheese.

Close the air fryer and cook for 1 minute, turn off the air fryer and let the eggplant to sit one more minute to allow the cheese melt fully.

INGREDIENTS

1 eggplant

1 egg, whisked

¼ cup Italian breadcrumbs

¼ cup grated Parmesan cheese

½ tsp garlic powder

½ tsp dried basil

½ cup marinara sauce

½ cup shredded mozzarella cheese

Tender LAMB CHOPS

READY IN **76 MIN**   SERVES **4**

INGREDIENTS

1 ¼ lb rack of lamb
(about 7-8 lamb
chops)

3 tbsp olive oil

1 tsp dried oregano

1 tsp garlic powder

1 tsp kosher salt

½ tsp black
pepper

DIRECTIONS

Pat the lamb rack dry. Remove silver skin
from the underside of ribs if needed. Cut into
individual chops.

In a large bowl, combine olive oil, oregano,
garlic powder, salt, & pepper. Add the lamb
and gently toss to coat in the marinade.
Cover and marinate for about 1 hour or up to
overnight in the refrigerator.

Preheat your air fryer to 380 degrees F.
Place lamb chops in the air fryer in a single
layer, making sure not to overlap the meat.

Air fry for 8 minutes, flip and fry for another
3-6 minutes, or to your preferred doneness.
Serve warm.

TIPS

Have leftovers? To reheat your lamb chops,
preheat your air fryer to 380 F. Then place
the leftover lamb chops in the air fryer and
cook for about 5 to 7 minutes, until
thoroughly warmed.

Delicious FRENCH BREAD PIZZA

READY IN 15 MIN   **SERVES 4**

This delicious French Bread Pizza is a favorite for the entire family! Not a fan of pepperoni?
No problem! Have a pizza night and let everyone choose their own toppings.

DIRECTIONS

Preheat your air fryer to 350 degrees.

Slice your french loaf in half and then cut lengthwise, giving
you 4 pieces. Depending on how long the bread is, you may
have to cut a little more off to fit in your air fryer.

Place two pieces of bread in the air fryer and fry for 2
minutes.

Carefully remove the loaf pieces and assemble your pizza
minus the pepperoni. Use about 2 tbsp of marinara sprinkled
with Italian seasoning. Top with cheese.

Cook for 4-5 minutes. Turn your air fryer off and open it.
Place pepperoni slices on the pizza, then close the air fryer
for about 1 minute to allow the pepperoni to melt into the
cheese.

Remove the pizza from the air fryer, allow 1-2 minutes to
cool, then enjoy!

INGREDIENTS

1 French Bread Loaf (Italian
bread will work too)

½ cup of marinara sauce

2 cups of shredded
mozzarella

1-2 tsp Italian Seasoning

Pepperoni for topping

89

Easy PIZZA BALLS

READY IN **25 MIN**   SERVES **2**

INGREDIENTS

1 can of
refrigerated
Pillsbury Classic
dough

½ cup cubed
mozzarella cheese

1 egg

1 tsp Italian
seasoning

½ cup marinara
sauce to serve

DIRECTIONS

Preheat the air fryer to 350 degrees F.

Unroll the dough and use a knife cut it into
square pieces.

Divide the mozzarella cubes and place some
in the center of each piece of dough. Then
make a ball shape by wrapping the cheese in
the dough.

Lightly spray the air fryer basket with cooking
spray, or line with air fryer parchment paper.

Arrange the pizza balls in the air fryer basket.
Whisk the egg in a cup, and use a pastry
brush to apply the balls with egg, then
sprinkle with herbs on top.

Cook the pizza balls in the air fryer for 20
minutes or until the balls will become
golden-brown and baked through.

Serve with marinara sauce and enjoy.

DELICIOUS
Air Fryer
SEAFOOD

Lemon Pepper SHRIMP

READY IN **13 MIN**   SERVES **4**

DIRECTIONS

Preheat your air fryer to 400°F.

Place the shrimp in a storage bag with olive oil, lemon juice, salt, and pepper.

Carefully combine all ingredients.

Add round parchment paper to the basket and place the raw shrimp inside the air fryer in one layer.

Cook for about 8 minutes, shaking the basket halfway through.

Remove the lemon pepper shrimp from the air fryer.

Serve with pasta, and enjoy!

TIPS

The shrimp are done when the shells turn pink, and the shrimp is just slightly white but still a little opaque.

INGREDIENTS

1 pound medium raw shrimp (peeled and deveined)

1/2 cup olive oil

2 tbsp lemon juice

1 tsp black pepper

½ tsp salt

8 oz. of pasta (cooked-optional)

Crispy
COCONUT SHRIMP

READY IN 25 MIN   **SERVES 5**

INGREDIENTS

½ cup all-purpose flour

1 tsp black pepper

½ tsp kosher salt

2 large eggs

¾ cup unsweetened flaked coconut

½ cup panko bread crumbs

12 oz. uncooked jumbo shrimp (peeled, deveined with tails on)

Fresh cilantro (for garnish)

Crispy coconut shrimp is a heavenly appetizer that will tantalize your taste buds. The crunchy, succulent shrimp are coated in a crispy, sweet, and salty coconut crust. Serve them at your next party and watch them disappear!

DIRECTIONS

In a shallow bowl, whisk together flour, pepper, and salt until well combined.

In a second bowl, lightly beat eggs.

Stir together coconut and bread crumbs in a third bowl.

Working one at a time, dredge each shrimp in flour mixture, shaking off any excess.

Dip the floured shrimp in the egg, allowing any excess to drip off.

Finally, press the shrimp into the coconut-bread crumb mixture, coating them well. Set the shrimp aside on a plate.

Spray the air fryer basket with cooking spray, then preheat it to 400°F.

Place shrimp in a single layer in the basket and air fry for 4 minutes.

Turn shrimp over and continue cooking until golden and fully cooked, 3-4 minutes.

Garnish with fresh cilantro and serve with your favorite dipping sauce.

Enjoy!

Bang Bang SHRIMP

READY IN 30 MIN   **SERVES 3-4**

INGREDIENTS

¾ cup mayonnaise

⅓ cup sweet chili sauce

1-3 tsp sriracha

1 ½ pound large shrimp (peeled and deveined with tail on)

⅔ cup cornstarch

½ cup buttermilk

2 cups panko breadcrumbs

½ tsp kosher salt

DIRECTIONS

In a small mixing bowl, combine mayonnaise, sweet chili sauce, and sriracha; set aside.

Place the cornstarch in a plastic zipped bag. Pour the buttermilk into a separate shallow bowl. In a third shallow bowl, mix the bread crumbs and salt.

Preheat the air fryer to 400°F.

Pat the shrimp dry and place them in the bag of cornstarch. Seal and shake the bag to coat the shrimp fully. Shake off any excess cornstarch and place the shrimp on a plate.

Dredge the shrimp in buttermilk, roll in the breadcrumbs, and press them firmly.

Place the coated shrimp in a single layer in the air fryer. Spray lightly with cooking spray.

Cook for 5 minutes, flip the shrimp, spray with cooking oil, and cook for another 5 minutes until fully cooked.

Remove from air fryer and lightly toss in bang bang sauce. Garnish with parsley and serve immediately.

Enjoy!

Crispy BREADED OYSTERS

READY IN **20 MIN**   SERVES **2**

INGREDIENTS

1 pound raw,
shucked oysters

½ cup all-purpose
flour

1 tsp cajun
seasoning

½ tsp kosher salt

¼ tsp black
pepper

1 large egg

1 tbsp milk

1 ½ cups panko
breadcrumbs

Lemon wedges

Melted garlic
butter

DIRECTIONS

Preheat your air fryer to 350°F.

Shuck and rinse the oysters, letting them
drain in a colander. Pat the shucked oysters
dry with paper towels.

In a shallow bowl, combine the flour, cajun
seasoning, salt, and pepper.

In a second bowl, whisk the egg and milk. In
a third bowl, add the panko breadcrumbs.

Dredge the oysters through the flour mixture,
dip in the egg mixture, then roll to coat in the
breadcrumbs.

Set the oysters in a single layer in the basket,
then spray lightly with cooking spray.

Cook in the air fryer for 4 minutes.

Flip the oysters, spray lightly with cooking oil
and cook for an additional 4 minutes.

Serve and enjoy!

Salt and Pepper
CALAMARI

READY IN **42 MIN**   SERVES **4**

INGREDIENTS

1 pound calamari rings
(patted dry)

1 lemon (juiced)

½ cup all-purpose flour

1 tsp garlic powder

2 egg whites

¼ cup milk

2 cup panko breadcrumbs

1 ½ tsp kosher salt

1 ½ tsp ground black pepper

FOR SERVING

sweet chili sauce

lemon wedges

Entertain your family and friends with this delicious, hot, and crispy homemade air fryer calamari dish. Serve with your favorite dipping sauce for a perfect appetizer or main course.

DIRECTIONS

Place the squid rings in a bowl with lemon juice and allow them to marinate for at least 30 minutes. Drain in a colander.

Place flour and garlic powder in a shallow bowl.

Whisk egg whites and milk together in a separate bowl.

Combine the panko breadcrumbs, salt, and pepper in a third bowl.

Coat the calamari rings first in flour, then in egg mixture, and finally in the panko breadcrumb mixture.

Preheat your air fryer to 400°F.

Place rings in the basket of the air fryer so that none are overlapping.

Spray the tops with EVO cooking spray.

Cook for 4 minutes.

Flip rings, spray with a little oil, and cook for an additional 3 minutes until opaque inside and fully cooked.

Serve and enjoy!

Crispy
BREADED SCALLOPS

READY IN **15 MIN**   SERVES **4**

INGREDIENTS

½ cup Italian breadcrumbs

½ tsp garlic powder

¼ tsp salt

½ tsp black pepper

2 tbsp butter (melted)

1 pound sea scallops (patted dry)

lemon wedges

Cook breaded scallops to golden perfection in less than 15 minutes using an air fryer. Serve with a lemon wedge for a delicious seafood dinner.

DIRECTIONS

Preheat your air fryer to 390°F.

In a shallow bowl, mix the breadcrumbs, garlic powder, salt, and pepper together.

Pour melted butter into a second shallow bowl.

Dredge each scallop through the melted butter, then roll in the breadcrumb mixture until they're completely coated; set aside on a plate.

Arrange scallops in a single layer, working in batches if necessary.

Air fry the scallops for 2 minutes.

Use tongs to carefully flip them over, then air fry for 3 more minutes until opaque and golden brown.

Serve with lemon wedges, and enjoy!

Bacon-Wrapped
SCALLOPS
READY IN **27 MIN**   SERVES **4-6**

INGREDIENTS

1 pound center-cut slices
of bacon

1 tsp honey

1 pound large sea scallops

3 tbsp melted butter

½ tsp Old Bay seasoning

salt and pepper (to taste)

¼ tsp red pepper flakes
(optional)

With this recipe, you can make air fryer bacon-wrapped scallops that are savory, tender, and delicious! Whether you're looking for an impressive dish to serve at a dinner party or something more casual for your family, these scallops will fit the bill.

DIRECTIONS

Brush your bacon strips with honey.

Place your bacon in your air fryer basket.

Cook it at 350°F for 5-7 minutes. Toss the bacon slices a few times to keep them moving.

Pat your scallops with a paper towel and season with salt and pepper.

Wrap your scallops with ½-1 slice of bacon.

Hold the bacon in place with a toothpick.

Melt your butter and incorporate the Old Bay seasoning, adding salt and pepper to taste.

Brush the butter mixture over your scallops.

Cook your scallops for 11-13 minutes. (The bacon should be crispy, and the scallops should be firm but slightly bounce back when you touch them.)

Sprinkle red pepper flakes over the top of them.

Serve and enjoy!

Marinated SALMON KABOBS

READY IN 35 MIN   **SERVES 2**

DIRECTIONS

Cut the salmon fillet into small cubes. Cut the onion into half rings and the lemon into regular rings.

Prepare the marinade by mixing the lemon zest, lemon juice, vinegar, olive oil, paprika, garlic powder, salt, and pepper. Roll the salmon cubes in the marinade, then let it sit for 10 minutes before adding chopped onion.

Thread the fish cubes, lemon, and onion pieces onto wooden kabob sticks.

Arrange the kabobs in the air fryer so that they are not touching, and cook at 350 degrees F for 15 minutes until the fish starts to turn golden.

Serve with your favorite greens and a sprinkle of herbs. Dill goes very well with this dish.

INGREDIENTS

1 lb salmon fillet

1 red onion

Zest from 1 lemon

1 tbsp lemon juice

1 tbsp wine or apple cider vinegar

2 tbsp olive oil

½ tsp paprika

Pinch of dried garlic powder

Salt and pepper to taste

Flavorful CRAB CAKES

READY IN **15 MIN**   SERVES **4**

Love crab cakes? Then you'll definitely want to give this air fryer recipe a
try! These fresh crab cakes are easy to make and come out perfectly crisp
every time.

DIRECTIONS

Preheat your air fryer to 370°F.

In a large bowl, add the lump crab meat, pepper, green
onions, mayonnaise, breadcrumbs, Old Bay Seasoning,
and lemon juice and mix until just combined.

Gently form four evenly-sized crab patties.

Place a piece of round parchment down inside the hot air
fryer, then carefully place each crab cake in the basket.

Cook the fresh crab cakes for 8-10 minutes until the crust
turns golden brown. Do not flip while cooking.

Remove the crab cakes from your air fryer and serve with
your favorite sauce and extra lemon on top.

Enjoy!

INGREDIENTS

8 oz. lump crab meat

1 red bell pepper (de-
seeded and chopped)

3 green onions
(chopped)

3 tbsp mayonnaise

3 tbsp breadcrumbs

2 tsp Old Bay
Seasoning

1 tsp lemon juice

lemon wedges

Crunchy CRAB RANGOON

READY IN **40 MIN**   SERVES **7**

INGREDIENTS

5 oz. cream cheese

5 oz. crab meat

2 green onions (chopped)

1 tsp Worcestershire sauce

1 ½ tsp garlic (minced)

salt and pepper (to taste)

olive oil cooking spray

28 wonton wrappers

water

DIRECTIONS

In a medium bowl, combine the cream cheese, crab meat, green onions, Worcestershire, minced garlic, and salt and pepper.

Place one wonton wrapper on a cutting board.

Brush the edges of the wrapper with water.

Fill the center of the wrapper with 1 ½ tsp of crab mixture.

Grab two opposite corners of the wrapper to come together in the middle to make a triangle. Take the other ends and bring them to the middle as well. Press to get all the air out and seal the seams together.

Spray the bottom of your air fryer and place your crab rangoons.

Spritz the tops of the rangoons with a little more cooking spray.

Bake at 360°F for 10 minutes. Check at the 5-minute mark and then every 2 minutes after to check on how brown and crispy you want them.

Serve with sweet chili sauce.

Enjoy!

Garlic Butter SALMON

READY IN **15 MIN**   SERVES **2**

DIRECTIONS

Preheat the air fryer to 360°F.

Season the fresh salmon with salt and pepper.

Mix together the melted butter, garlic, and parsley in a bowl.

Baste the salmon fillets with the garlic butter mixture and carefully place the salmon inside the basket side-by-side with the skin side down.

Cook for approximately 10 minutes until salmon flakes easily with a knife or fork.

Eat immediately and enjoy!

TIPS

You can store this air-fried salmon for up to 3 days. When ready to eat, reheat salmon in a preheated air fryer set at 370°F for approximately 4 minutes.

INGREDIENTS

2 6 oz. boneless, skin-on salmon fillets (preferably wild-caught)

2 tbsp butter (melted)

1 tsp garlic (minced)

1 tsp fresh Italian parsley (chopped or ¼ teaspoon dried)

salt and pepper (to taste)

Keto-Friendly TILAPIA

READY IN 15 MIN   **SERVES 3-4**

If you're in need of a healthy, home-cooked meal but short on time, try this air fryer tilapia. This dish takes less than 20 minutes to make and is just as delicious with fresh or frozen fish fillets! Perfect for the keto diet.

DIRECTIONS

Preheat your air fryer to 400°F.

Place the tilapia fillets on a large plate and drizzle with olive oil.

In a small bowl, mix the paprika, garlic powder, onion powder, salt, and pepper.

Sprinkle seasoning evenly over the fillets, then place in a single layer in the air fryer.

Cook tilapia for 10 minutes, flipping halfway through. Remove the tilapia from the air fryer.

Serve with lemon wedges, and enjoy!

INGREDIENTS

4 tilapia fillets

2 tbsp olive oil

½ tsp paprika

½ tsp garlic powder

½ tsp onion powder

½ tsp salt

½ tsp black pepper

lemon wedges
(optional)

Panko-Crusted MAHI MAHI

READY IN **17 MIN**   SERVES **3-4**

DIRECTIONS

Preheat your air fryer to 400°F.

Place the Mahi Mahi fillets on a large plate and drizzle with olive oil.

In a shallow dish, mix the panko breadcrumbs, paprika, garlic powder, onion powder, salt, and pepper.

Dip each Mahi Mahi fillet into the panko mixture, then place it in a single layer in the air fryer basket.

Spritz with cooking oil.

Cook for 12 to 15 minutes, flipping the fish halfway through cooking.

Remove them from the air fryer.

Serve with lemon wedges, and enjoy!

INGREDIENTS

1 to 1 ½ pounds Mahi Mahi fillets

2 tbsp olive oil

2 cups panko breadcrumbs

1 tsp paprika

½ tsp garlic powder

½ tsp onion powder

½ tsp salt

½ tsp pepper

Flakey DILL COD FISH

READY IN **20 MIN**   SERVES **4**

INGREDIENTS

4 cod fillets

4 tbsp butter
(melted)

6 garlic cloves
(minced)

1 lemon

1 tsp dried dill (or 2
tbsp fresh dill,
chopped)

½ tsp salt

DIRECTIONS

Preheat your air fryer to 370°F.

Mix the butter, garlic, lemon juice, dill, and
salt in a bowl.

Add a cod loin into the bowl, coating it
completely.

Lightly press the garlic into the cod and
repeat with the remaining cod fillets.

Place all the cod pieces into the air fryer in
one layer.

Cook for 10 minutes, then carefully remove
from the air fryer.

Garnish the cod with more lemon juice or
butter.

Enjoy!

Asian AHI TUNA STEAKS

READY IN **24 MIN**   SERVES **2**

Forget about Bonefish Grill! This air fryer Asian ahi tuna recipe rivals any
restaurant, and it's so easy to make at home. The tuna steaks are marinated
in simple soy, ginger, and honey mixture, then air fried to perfection.

DIRECTIONS

In a bowl, combine the soy sauce, honey sesame oil, fresh
ginger, and rice vinegar. Mix well!

Add the tuna steaks and let them marinate for 20 minutes
to 2 hours.

Lightly grease the air fryer basket with an oil spray.
Place the marinated tuna steaks in the basket, shaking off
as much marinade as possible, in a single layer.

Air fry at 380°F for 4 minutes.

Let it rest on the cutting board for a minute before slicing.

Garnish with sliced green onion and sesame seeds and
serve immediately with soy sauce for dipping.

TIPS

If using frozen fillets: You can either thaw them in the fridge
overnight (recommended) or place the frozen tuna steaks in
a greased air fryer basket and air fry at 380 for 3 minutes.
This will thaw out the tuna but will not cook it.

INGREDIENTS

2 (6 oz.) boneless,
skinless yellowfin tuna
steaks (preferably wild-
caught)

¼ cup soy sauce

2 tsp honey

1 tsp sesame oil

1 tsp fresh ginger (finely
grated)

½ tsp rice vinegar
(substitute any vinegar
of choice)

sliced green onions (for
garnish)

sesame seeds (for
garnish)

Blackened CATFISH

READY IN **60 MIN**   SERVES **2**

INGREDIENTS

2 catfish fillets

1 cup milk (or buttermilk)

½ tbsp olive oil

1 ½ tbsp blackening seasoning (or Cajun seasoning)

½ tsp dried oregano

½ tsp kosher salt

½ tsp black pepper

½ tsp garlic powder

¼ tsp cayenne pepper

lemon wedges

fresh chopped parsley

DIRECTIONS

At least 30 minutes before cooking, place the catfish fillets in a plastic zipper bag or large bowl and pour the milk (or buttermilk) over it, allowing it to soak to remove the fishy flavor.

In a small bowl, combine the blackening or Cajun seasoning, oregano, salt, pepper, garlic powder, and cayenne pepper, then set it aside.

When ready to cook, preheat your air fryer to 400°F.

Remove the fish and pat it dry. Drizzle the fillets with olive oil. Sprinkle the spice mixture onto both sides of each fillet, coating them completely.

Place the fillets in a single layer inside. Spray the tops of the fish.

Air fry for 10 minutes.

Carefully flip the fish and fry for another 10 to 12 minutes (20 to 22 minutes total) until it reaches your desired doneness.

Serve with lemon wedges and garnished with parsley.

Enjoy!

Juicy
SALMON PATTIES

READY IN 25 MIN   **SERVES 5**

INGREDIENTS

10 oz. raw salmon (skinless and boneless)

2 green onions (finely chopped)

1 tbsp fresh dill (finely chopped)

½ tsp salt

½ tsp freshly ground pepper

1 egg (lightly beaten)

3 tbsp almond flour

These juicy salmon patties are delicious, easy to make, and perfect for a healthy weeknight meal! Thanks to the air fryer, they cook up quickly with little oil and make a great alternative to traditional burgers.

DIRECTIONS

Preheat the air fryer to 370°F.

Place the salmon in a food processor and pulse a few times until it resembles ground meat.

Transfer to a large bowl.

Add the onions, dill, salt, pepper, egg, and almond flour.

Stir well until everything is well combined.

Create 5 balls and use the back of your hand to flatten them.

Cook for 15 minutes, flipping the patties after 8 minutes.

Serve warm with sour cream, tarter sauce, or any preferred dip.

Enjoy!

TIPS

If you don't have any cooked salmon on hand, you can use canned salmon instead. Just make sure to drain it well before mixing it with the other ingredients.

Crunchy
FISH TACOS

READY IN **25 MIN**   SERVES **2**

INGREDIENTS

1 pack taco shells

1 pound cod fish

1 tbsp olive oil

½ tsp ground black pepper

¼ tsp garlic powder

pinch of salt

2 tbsp bread crumbs

1 avocado

2 tomatoes

1 red pepper

1 red onion

greens (parsley, green onion, lettuce)

sauces (taco sauce, cheese sauce, tartar sauce)

These air fryer fish tacos are healthy, easy to make, and full of flavor! The perfect main course for your next Mexican-inspired meal.

DIRECTIONS

Preheat the air fryer to 400°F.

In a small mixing bowl, combine olive oil, black pepper, garlic, salt, and bread crumbs.

Cut the fish fillet into big pieces. Put in the bowl with the oil and spice mixture. Mix well!

Put the piece of parchment paper in the air fryer basket. Arrange fish fillets on it in one layer.

Bake for 15-20 minutes until golden brown crust.

Take out fish fillet, let cool, and cut into small bite pieces.

Fill taco shells with fish bites, tomatoes, greens, onion, avocado, and red pepper.

Top with your favorite taco sauce.

Enjoy!

TIPS

Warm up the taco shells in the air fryer for a few minutes before adding fish and toppings. It will make them crunchy.

Bite-Sized FISH NUGGETS

READY IN **25 MIN**   SERVES **2-3**

DIRECTIONS

Preheat the air fryer to 400°F.

Mix the almond flour, pepper, and salt together.

Coat the fish pieces with flour mixture, dip into the beaten eggs, and then cover with pork rinds.

Arrange the nuggets in the air fryer basket in a single layer.

Cook for 10 minutes and flip them over.

Bake for 5 additional minutes.

Serve with homemade mayo.

Enjoy!

TIPS

This fish nugget recipe is perfect for the keto diet.

I made this using perch. However, you can swap it out for another type of fish, such as cod, halibut, or tilapia.

Use breadcrumbs in place of almond flour if you'd like!

INGREDIENTS

½ cup almond flour

1 tsp salt

1 tsp freshly ground pepper

1 lb white fish (cut into bite-size pieces)

12 eggs (beaten)

1 cup pork rinds (ground)

½ cup homemade mayo (optional)

Crispy FISH STICKS

READY IN **20 MIN**   SERVES **2-3**

DIRECTIONS

Preheat the air fryer at 400°F.

Place the flour on a plate.

Mix together the breadcrumbs and paprika.

Season the fish with salt, pepper, lemon juice, and garlic.

Dredge the sticks in the flour, dip them into the beaten eggs, and coat them with a breadcrumb mixture.

Cook for 5 minutes, flip over and then cook for 5 minutes more.

Whisk together the mayo and Piri Piri and serve on the side.

Enjoy!

INGREDIENTS

½ cup all-purpose flour

1 ½ tsp sweet paprika

1 cup breadcrumbs

2 eggs (beaten)

1 lb white cod fillet (cut into sticks)

½ tsp salt

½ tsp freshly ground pepper

1 tsp lemon juice

½ tsp garlic powder

½ cup homemade mayo (optional)

2 tsp Piri Piri sauce (optional)

DELICIOUS
Air Fryer
SIDE DISHES

Creamy BROCCOLI + CHEESE

READY IN 25 MIN   **SERVES 2**

This iconic combination is a classic for a reason. This creamy, cheesy broccoli
dish is the perfect way to get practically anyone to eat his or her vegetables.

DIRECTIONS

Preheat the air fryer to 400 F.

Bring a pot of salted water to a boil. Add the broccoli
florets and cook for 3-4 minutes. Remove from the
boiling water and transfer to an oven-proof dish that fits
the air fryer or an air fryer cake accessory.

In a bowl, whisk together the heavy cream, cheddar,
cream cheese, garlic, pepper, and salt. Pour the mixture
over the broccoli florets.

Air fry for 12-15 minutes, stirring every 5 minutes.

INGREDIENTS

1 broccoli head, cut into
florets

½ cup heavy cream

⅓ cup cheddar,
shredded

3 tbsp cream cheese

½ tsp garlic powder

½ tsp freshly ground
pepper

½ tsp salt

Charred
SHISHITO PEPPERS

READY IN **11 MIN**   SERVES **4**

INGREDIENTS

8 ounces shishito peppers, washed and thoroughly dried

2 tsp olive oil

½ cup mayo

1 tbsp lemon juice, plus more for drizzling

½ tsp coarse salt

½ tsp paprika

¼ tsp garlic powder

Air fryer shishito peppers come together with a few simple ingredients. Charred, crispy, and filled with flavor, it's the best app ever!

DIRECTIONS

Preheat your air fryer to 390 F.

Toss peppers with oil in a large bowl until evenly coated.

Place in an even layer in the preheated air fryer basket and cook for 6 minutes, shaking the basket halfway through.

While the peppers are roasting, prepare a dipping sauce by mixing together the mayo, lemon juice, paprika, and garlic powder until well combined.

Transfer the cooked peppers to a platter, drizzle lemon juice over top, and sprinkle with salt.

Enjoy immediately with dipping sauce.

Garlic BREAD

READY IN **12 MIN** SERVES **4**

INGREDIENTS

1 half loaf of bread

3 tablespoons
butter, softened

3 garlic cloves,
minced

½ teaspoon Italian
seasoning

small pinch of red
pepper flakes

¼ cup shredded
mozzarella cheese
(optional)

Freshly grated
parmesan cheese
(optional)

Parsley for
serving/topping
(optional)

DIRECTIONS

Preheat your air fryer to 350 degrees.

Cut the bread in half or whatever size is
needed to fit in your air fryer.

Mix the softened butter, garlic, Italian
seasoning, and red pepper flakes in a bowl.

Baste the garlic butter mixture on top of the
bread evenly.

Place the garlic bread in the air fryer side by
side and cook for about 6 to 7 minutes. If
using cheese, add the cheese with just 1 to 2
minutes left to cook.

Remove the garlic bread from your air fryer,
slice, and serve!

Fluffy CORNBREAD

READY IN **21 MIN**   SERVES **4**

DIRECTIONS

Spray an air fryer pan with cooking spray; set aside.

In a large mixing bowl, add the cornbread mix, egg and milk; mix well.

Transfer the batter to the prepared pan and air fry at 320 degrees F for 12 minutes. After that time, cover the pan with aluminum foil, then continue air frying for another 4-5 minutes until cooked through.

INGREDIENTS

1 package Jiffy Cornbread

1 large egg

⅓ cup milk

CORNBREAD MUFFINS

Don't want to deal with cutting the full cornbread into slices? Why not make cornbread muffins instead! To do so, you'll need silicone muffin cups.

Spray the cups to prevent the batter from sticking, then fill them about ¾ of the way full. This will prevent your batter from spilling over the sides as it bakes. Only fill as many cups as you can fit in your fryer at one time.

Because they are smaller, these muffins will cook faster than the larger one-pan version. Make sure to keep an eye on them and use a toothpick to check for doneness.

If the tops are looking golden, but the insides are still wet, you can cover them with tinfoil and continue cooking.

Crunchy ZUCCHINI CHIPS

READY IN **18 MIN**   SERVES **4**

Air fryer zucchini chips are a fresh, crisp, and delish way to enjoy seasonal
flavors! In less than 20 minutes, you'll have a whole batch of crunchy chips
with no oil, salt, or harmful additives.

DIRECTIONS

Cut zucchini into thin slices, approximately ¼ inches.

Mix panko breadcrumbs, garlic powder, and onion
powder in a bowl.

Whisk one egg into a separate bowl and put the flour
in a third bowl.

Dip zucchini into the flour, then the egg, then the
breadcrumbs.

Place the breaded zucchini in an air fryer in a single
layer and cook at 380 degrees for 7-9 minutes,
flipping halfway.

Enjoy immediately.

INGREDIENTS

1 medium-sized zucchini

½ cup panko
breadcrumbs

½ tsp garlic powder

¼ tsp onion powder

1 egg

3 tbsp flour

Fried
PICKLES

READY IN **16 MIN**   SERVES **4**

INGREDIENTS

36 large pickle slices

1 cup Panko bread crumbs

1 large egg

½ tbsp water

½ cup all-purpose flour

½ tsp garlic powder

½ tsp paprika

½ tsp dried dill

Looking for a perfect snack or appetizer? These air fryer fried pickles are crunchy on the outside and hot and juicy on the inside. The crunch is so satisfying—you won't be able to resist! Even better? These can be ready in less than 20 minutes!

DIRECTIONS

Drain pickles completely, and lay them on a few layers of paper towels, drying them well.

Preheat the air fryer to 400 degrees F.

In a wide, shallow bowl, place Panko crumbs. In a second bowl, whisk the egg with water. In a third bowl, whisk together the flour, garlic powder, paprika, and dill.

Dredge each pickle through the flour mixture, dip them in the egg, then press them into the Panko to coat.

Carefully place a single layer of pickles in the basket. Work in batches as necessary. Lightly spray the tops of the pickles with cooking spray, then cook for 4 minutes. Flip the pickles and cook them for an additional 2-4 minutes until they're browned and crispy.

Allow to cool slightly before serving with your favorite dipping sauce.

TO SERVE

No fried pickle is complete without a dipping sauce. Besides the classic pairing of ranch dressing, here are a few other ideas to try. I highly recommend dipping these pickles in a combination of blue cheese dressing and buffalo sauce. Another great option is this honey siracha sauce—it's delicious, and the sweet-spicy flavor works wonderfully with salty pickles. Want a twist on a classic? Give this Sriracha Ranch sauce a try. You'll love it!

Pasta CHIPS

READY IN **35 MIN**   SERVES **4**

INGREDIENTS

8 oz farfalle pasta

½ cup parmesan, grated

1 tbsp olive oil

½ tsp dried oregano

½ tsp dried basil

½ tsp garlic powder

½ tsp salt

½ tsp freshly ground pepper

Marinara sauce, to serve (optional)

DIRECTIONS

Boil the pasta according to the package instructions and drain.

In a large bowl, combine the farfalle, parmesan, oil, oregano, basil, garlic, salt, and pepper. Toss to coat.

Air fry at 400 degrees for 12-15 minutes, stirring from time to time so they cook evenly.

Serve with marinara sauce, if desired.

Cheesy KALE CHIPS

READY IN **39 MIN**   SERVES **4**

You won't be able to resist these crispy-crunchy 5-ingredient air fryer kale chips! The nutritional yeast gives them a cheesy flavor while keeping them totally vegan.

DIRECTIONS

Wash your kale leaves and lie them to dry on paper towels (or dry them with a salad spinner).

Next, place the leaves on a cutting board and cut down the sides of the stalk. Take the two leaves and tear them into smaller pieces, and discard the stalk.

Place them in a bowl and drizzle olive oil over your kale. Using your hands, massage the oil evenly onto all of the kale pieces.

Sprinkle the nutritional yeast, salt, and pepper and toss to coat.

Place your kale in the basket, as close to a single layer as possible. You will be cooking in batches.

Cook for 5-7 minutes at 270 degrees, tossing the kale chips every 3 minutes to prevent burning.

INGREDIENTS

½ bunch of kale

2 tbsp of olive oil

1 tbsp of nutritional yeast

¼ teaspoon of sea salt

⅛ teaspoon of pepper

Crunchy
GREEN BEAN FRIES

READY IN **15 MIN**   SERVES **3-4**

INGREDIENTS

6 oz fresh raw green beans

1 egg

1 egg white

½ cup panko crumbs, divided

2 tbsp grated parmesan

½ tbsp garlic powder

1 tsp paprika

¼ tsp salt

⅛ tsp ground black pepper

Need a quick veggie side the whole family will love? These air fryer green bean fries are irresistibly crispy, easy to prep, and ready in less than 20 minutes!

DIRECTIONS

Preheat your air fryer to 400 degrees F and wash and trim your green beans.

Whisk your egg and egg white in a medium bowl.

In a small bowl, use the back of a large spoon and crush ¼ cup of panko crumbs as fine as you can. These smaller crumbs will help coat all of your green beans.

In a wide dish, combine the crushed panko and the remaining ¼ cup of panko crumbs, parmesan, and seasoning.

Place a few green beans in the egg wash, making sure to coat it well. Use a fork to lift them out, shaking any excess egg off. Place it in the panko and use your fingers to cover the green bean, flipping it over on all sides to get as much covered as possible.

Lay your breaded green beans in the basket. Leave room around them to allow them to get nice and crispy. Place them in the air fryer and set the temperature to 400 degrees. Cook for 4 to 5 minutes and then check them.

Serve green bean fries on their own or with your favorite dipping sauce.

Crispy SWEET POTATO FRIES

READY IN 20 MIN   **SERVES 4**

DIRECTIONS

Peel, then cut sweet potatoes into ½-inch strips to create fries.

Coat sweet potato fries with olive oil.

Add in the fine sea salt, garlic powder, and paprika and mix to combine the seasoning evenly.

Cook the sweet potato fries at 380 degrees for 15-18 minutes, shaking the basket every 5 minutes.

INGREDIENTS

2 medium sweet potatoes

1 tbsp olive oil

½ tsp fine sea salt

½ tsp garlic powder

¼ tsp paprika

TIPS

Want extra-crispy fries? Here are a few helpful tips to help you get them!

First, make sure to cut your wedges thin. The thinner they are, the more crispy they will be.

Second, get rid of any excess moisture by patting your sweet potatoes with a paper towel before placing them in your air fryer basket. You want to get them as dry as possible before air frying.

Lastly, make sure your sweet potato fries have proper airflow in the fryer by not overcrowding the basket.

Crispy + Fluffy
POTATO WEDGES

READY IN **55 MIN**   SERVES **4**

INGREDIENTS

4 russet potatoes

1 tbsp olive oil

2 tsp garlic powder

1 tsp salt

¼ tsp pepper

½ tsp smoked paprika

¼ cup grated parmesan

optional: 1 tbsp fresh parsley

Crispy on the outside and fluffy on the inside, these perfectly-seasoned air fryer potato wedges are sure to be a hit with the entire family. Air fried to crispy perfection, these wedges are finished with parmesan for an irresistible side dish!

DIRECTIONS

Thoroughly wash your potatoes. Cut them into wedges. Do this by cutting them lengthwise, then lay them on the flat side, and cut them again lengthwise. Then, cut once more lengthwise.

Place them in a large bowl, covering the potatoes with water and then topping it with ice. Let them soak in the ice bath for 30 minutes.

Remove the wedges from the ice bath and pat dry with paper towels. Place them back in a dry bowl and drizzle them with olive oil and the seasonings (garlic powder, salt, pepper, and paprika).

Preheat the air fryer to 400 degrees and place the seasoned wedges in the basket in a single layer. Cook for 15 minutes, flipping them regularly, about every 5 minutes.

Once they are cooked to desired crispiness, remove the wedges and toss them with the parmesan and garnish with parsley.

Serve them with your favorite dipping sauce.

Crispy
ONION RINGS

INGREDIENTS

1 large sweet (Vidalia) onion, sliced into ½-inch rings

2 large eggs

⅔ cup buttermilk

⅔ cup all-purpose flour

½ tsp kosher salt

½ tsp black pepper

½ tsp garlic powder

1 ½ cups panko bread crumbs

These air fryer onion rings are crispy perfection! Just slice, dredge, then air fry for the best onion rings ever in less than 30 minutes.

DIRECTIONS

Peel onion and cut it into ½-inch thick slices. Separate the slices and place them on a plate. Set aside.

In a wide, shallow bowl, lightly beat the eggs with the buttermilk until well combined. In a second bowl, combine the flour, salt, pepper, and garlic powder. Place the panko bread crumbs in a third bowl.

Dip each onion ring into the flour, then the buttermilk mixture, and then dredge it through the bread crumbs, pressing to adhere. Set aside on a baking sheet and repeat with the remaining rings. Spray the rings with an EVO Oil sprayer.

Preheat the air fryer to 380 degrees F.

Transfer the rings into the air fryer basket in a single layer, nesting the smaller ones inside the larger ones but leaving a little space between each ring. Don't overcrowd the basket, and work in batches if necessary.

Air fry for 9-12 minutes or until golden brown and crispy.

Sprinkle with salt if desired, and serve.

Crisp FRENCH FRIES

READY IN **30 MIN**   SERVES **4**

These crispy air-fried french fries are made within 30 minutes and pair
perfectly with almost anything. Enjoy a deep-fried flavor burst with little to
no oil, thanks to the air fryer.

DIRECTIONS

Fill a medium-sized bowl halfway with cold water.

Peel potatoes (if desired) and cut them into 1/4 inch slices.

As you slice the potatoes, add them into the water to soak.

Drain potatoes and fill the bowl back up. Mix the potatoes
around like you're tossing a salad with your hands. Drain
again. Repeat 5-6 times until the water is clear.

Dry off potatoes and bowl with a paper towel.

Add potatoes back to the dry bowl. Add extra virgin olive
oil and salt. Mix to combine.

Cook french fries at 350 degrees for 10 minutes, then at 400
degrees for 15-18 minutes, shaking the basket every 5
minutes.

INGREDIENTS

2 russet potatoes

1 tbsp extra virgin olive oil

⅛ tsp salt

Garlic Parmesan FRIES

READY IN 35 MIN   **SERVES 2**

INGREDIENTS

3 large potatoes

1 tbsp extra virgin olive oil

1 tbsp melted butter

1 tbsp granulated garlic

½ tsp ground black pepper

½ tsp salt

½ cup shredded parmesan cheese

DIRECTIONS

Preheat the air fryer to 350 degrees.

Peel and cut potatoes into fries. Try to cut them into as similar sizes as possible, as that will give you an even cook. Then, pat the potatoes dry with a paper towel.

Place the cut potatoes in a mixing bowl and pour in the oil. Add salt, pepper, and garlic, then mix until the fries are completely coated.

Place the fries in the air fryer basket and cook for 10 minutes. Shake the fries, then increase the temperature to 400 degrees for 15 to 18 minutes, shaking the basket every 5 minutes.

Remove fries from the basket when golden brown. Top with parmesan and serve immediately.

Twice-Baked
POTATOES

READY IN 60 MIN   **SERVES 6**

These twice-baked potatoes come out crispy on the outside and fluffy on the inside. An excellent side dish or appetizer, these potatoes are a crowd-pleaser every single time.

INGREDIENTS

3 potatoes, rinsed

½ cup cheddar, shredded

3 tbsp sour cream

½ tsp salt

½ tsp freshly ground pepper

½ tsp garlic powder

3 slices bacon, cooked, crumbled

1 tbsp fresh parsley, chopped

DIRECTIONS

Place the potatoes in the air fryer basket and bake at 400F for 40-45 minutes, until soft. Let them cool for 10-15 minutes.

Then, slice them into halves lengthwise. Scoop out the flesh, leaving enough so the skins don't break.

In a large bowl, mix together the potato flesh, cheddar, sour cream, salt, pepper, garlic powder, and bacon. Divide the mixture between the potato halves.

Air fry again at 400F, for 5-7 minutes.

Top with fresh parsley and serve.

Smashed POTATOES

READY IN **47 MIN**   SERVES **4**

You only need a handful of ingredients and less than an hour to make these irresistible smashed potatoes in the air fryer! This delectable side will have everyone reaching for seconds.

DIRECTIONS

Wash and scrub your potatoes. Place them in a pot filled with cold water. Bring the water to a boil.

Boil the potatoes till they are tender enough to be poked with a fork, about 15-20 minutes.

Combine your olive oil and garlic. Then preheat your air fryer to 400 degrees.

Drain your potatoes, then smash them slightly using a fork. Brush them with olive oil and garlic and sprinkle salt and pepper on top of them. Gently place them in your air fryer with a little room around each of them to allow full crispiness.

Cook for 10-13 minutes until they are nice and crispy. Top with parsley if desired, and serve. Adjust time for larger potatoes or different air fryers.

INGREDIENTS

24-ounce bag of baby red potatoes

2 tbsp olive oil

1 tbsp minced garlic

salt and pepper to taste

Fluffy BAKED POTATOES

READY IN **60 MIN**   SERVES **4**

INGREDIENTS

4 medium russet
potatoes

1 tbsp olive oil

Sea salt, to taste

Optional, to serve
with potatoes:
butter, sour cream,
crumbled bacon,
cheese, chives,
black pepper

DIRECTIONS

Preheat your air fryer to 400 degrees F.

Rinse and scrub the potatoes, then
thoroughly dry with a paper towel.

Rub the skin with olive oil and sprinkle with
salt (and pepper if desired).

Air fry the potatoes at 400 degrees F for 40-
50 minutes, using tongs to flip them once
halfway through the cooking time.

Serve warm with your favorite toppings.

TOPPINGS

Want even more topping ideas? Try a twist
on a classic by topping your potato with
broccoli and cheese. Or, make it a loaded
potato with leftover meat such as pulled
pork, shredded chicken, or beef. Why not
try a potato Mexican style with pico de
gallo, avocado, black beans, jalapenos, taco
meat, and a squeeze of sour cream?

Fluffy RICE

READY IN **35 MIN**   SERVES **2**

INGREDIENTS

1 cup jasmine rice

1 tbsp olive oil, or butter

1 ½ cups water

½ tsp salt

DIRECTIONS

Preheat your air fryer to 350 degrees F.

Place the rice in a colander and rinse several times until the water runs clear.

Meanwhile, combine the water, oil (or butter), and salt in a large measuring cup and heat it in the microwave for 3 and a half minutes.

Transfer the rinsed rice to a 6-inch air fryer pan or cake pan. Pour the water over the rice and swirl the pan. Tightly cover the pan with a piece of aluminum foil, then place it in the air fryer basket.

Cook rice for 25 minutes.

Check that water has been absorbed, adding an additional 3 to 5 minutes if necessary. Allow to sit for 10 minutes, then fluff with a fork and serve.

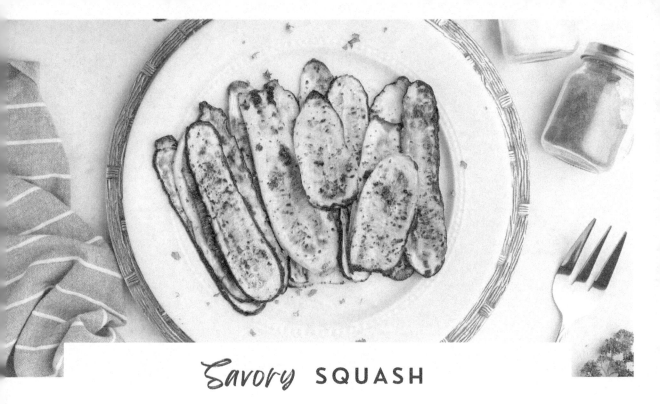

Savory SQUASH

READY IN 15 MIN   **SERVES 4**

This air fryer squash recipe is easy, versatile, and positively scrumptious. It is packed with both nutrition and flavor that the whole family will enjoy.

DIRECTIONS

Preheat your air fryer to 400 degrees.

Wash your vegetables. Cut them lengthwise as close to ¼ to ½ inch as you can. You definitely don't want thinner than ¼ of an inch or larger than ½.

Drizzle your olive oil and sprinkle your seasoning on your vegetables. Slightly toss them to evenly coat them.

Lay them in your air fryer basket. It is okay if they slightly overlap.

Cook them at 400 degrees for 10 minutes. Check it at 8 minutes for your thinner sliced ones, and then continue cooking till they are golden brown and crispy. Season with salt and pepper if desired and serve.

Continue with your next batch, if needed.

INGREDIENTS

2 squashes

2 zucchinis

1 tbsp McCormick's salt-free vegetable seasoning

2 tsp garlic-infused olive oil (or regular olive oil)

Salt and pepper to taste

Parmesan SPAGHETTI SQUASH

READY IN 30 MIN   **SERVES 4**

Spaghetti squash is roasted in the air fryer and topped with parmesan
cheese for a simple vegetable side dish.

DIRECTIONS

Preheat your air fryer to 360 degrees.

Cut the ends off of the spaghetti squash and slice it in
half lengthwise. Remove the seeds with a spoon or
melon baller.

Place the spaghetti squash in the air fryer side by side,
cutting the long sides down if needed slightly to fit.

Cook for 25-30 minutes, then remove the spaghetti
squash from the air fryer.

Season with salt and pepper and comb down the sides
of the squash to create spaghetti-like strands. Add in
Parmesan cheese and mix.

Enjoy!

INGREDIENTS

1 spaghetti squash

salt and pepper to taste

½ cup grated parmesan
cheese

Honey BUTTERNUT SQUASH

READY IN **25 MIN**   SERVES **4**

INGREDIENTS

1 butternut squash, peeled, seeds removed, and cut into 1-inch chunks

2 tbsp oil

2 tbsp honey

½ tsp ground cinnamon

¼ tsp fine sea salt

1 tsp honey (for drizzling on top)

DIRECTIONS

Preheat your air fryer to 400 degrees.

Place cubed butternut squash pieces, oil, honey, ground cinnamon, and sea salt into a bowl and mix to combine.

Add butternut squash mixture to the air fryer (do not fill more than halfway) and cook for 14-16 minutes until tender, shaking the basket every 5 minutes or so. You will know the squash is done when you can easily pierce a fork through it.

Place in serving dish and drizzle additional honey on top.

Enjoy immediately.

Maple-Roasted ACORN SQUASH

READY IN **20 MIN**   SERVES **4**

Acorn squash is my absolute favorite! It has a lightly sweet taste and complements many different flavors, including maple syrup. This recipe pairs the two beautifully.

DIRECTIONS

Preheat the air fryer to 380 degrees.

Cut acorn squash in half and scoop out pulp and seeds.

Cut halves into 1-inch slices.

Spread oil on both sides of the slices and place in the fryer in a single layer.

Baste maple syrup on top of each acorn squash slice.

Sprinkle sea salt on top evenly.

Bake for 10-12 minutes until a fork pierces it easily.

Enjoy immediately or keep refrigerated for up to 3 days reheating prior to serving.

INGREDIENTS

1 acorn squash

1 tbsp olive oil

2 tbsp maple syrup

1/8 tsp coarse sea salt

Cubed SWEET POTATOES

READY IN **20 MIN**   SERVES **3**

Air fried sweet potato cubes are an easy-to-make side dish that requires next to
no prep work. All you'll have to do is cube, season, and air fry for 10 minutes!

DIRECTIONS

Preheat your air fryer to 400 F.

Peel and slice the sweet potato into ½ inch cubes, you
should have 2-2 ½ cups of sweet potato cubes.

Place sweet potato cubes into a large mixing bowl,
drizzle with oil and sprinkle seasonings, then toss to
combine.

Add the seasoned sweet potato to the air fryer, then
cook for 8-10 minutes, shaking the basket halfway
through.

Sprinkle with parsley (if using) and serve warm.

INGREDIENTS

1 large sweet potato, or
two medium ones

1 tbsp olive oil

1 tsp brown sugar
(optional)

½ tsp salt

½ tsp dried parsley

Fresh parsley for garnish
(optional)

Brussels Sprouts & SWEET POTATOES

READY IN **23 MIN**   SERVES **4-6**

Tender sweet potato cubes are paired with slightly charred Brussels sprouts for
a healthy, flavorful side dish that works well with any protein.

DIRECTIONS

Preheat air fryer to 360 degrees.

Peel and dice sweet potatoes into 1-inch pieces.

Mix the diced sweet potatoes with 1 tablespoon of oil
and cook in air fryer for 5-6 minutes.

Meanwhile, trim and cut Brussels sprouts and mix with 2
tablespoons oil, minced garlic, salt, pepper, and red
pepper flakes.

Increase temperature to 400 degrees and add Brussels
Sprouts to air fryer with the sweet potatoes.

Mix to combine and cook for 8 minutes, shaking basket
halfway.

INGREDIENTS

1 pound brussels sprouts

2 sweet potatoes, cubed

3 tbsp oil

2 cloves garlic, minced

½ teaspoon salt

Pepper to taste

Small pinch of red
pepper flakes

Bacon BRUSSELS SPROUTS

READY IN **40 MIN**   SERVES **4**

INGREDIENTS

8 slices bacon

1 lb brussels
sprouts, trimmed

1 tbsp olive oil

½ tsp kosher salt

½ tsp black pepper

Balsamic glaze

DIRECTIONS

Add the bacon in a single layer to the air
fryer basket. Cook at 400 degrees F for 10
minutes, turning halfway through, until the
bacon is mostly cooked but still soft.

Meanwhile, cut the brussels sprouts in half
lengthwise (or quarters if they're very large)
and place them in a large bowl. Drizzle them
with olive oil, tossing to coat. Sprinkle with
salt and pepper.

When the timer is up, remove the bacon and
chop it into small pieces. Add the bacon to
the bowl with the brussels sprouts and toss.

Discard any excess grease from the air fryer,
then add the contents of the bowl to the
basket.

Cook at 400 degrees F for 20-25 minutes,
shaking the basket every 5-10 minutes to
ensure they are evenly browned.

Use a slotted spoon to transfer the brussels
and bacon to a serving bowl, then drizzle
with the desired amount of balsamic glaze, or
serve it on the side.

Cheesy ASPARAGUS

READY IN **10 MIN**   SERVES **4**

INGREDIENTS

1 bundle asparagus

1 tsp olive oil

⅛ tsp garlic salt

1 tbsp parmesan cheese (powdered or grated)

pepper to taste

DIRECTIONS

Preheat your air fryer to 400 degrees.

Clean asparagus and pat dry. Cut 1 inch off the bottom to take off the woody stems.

Lay asparagus in a single layer in the air fryer and spritz with oil.

Sprinkle garlic salt evenly on top of the asparagus. Season with pepper, and then add a little Parmesan cheese across the top.

Cook at 400 degrees for 7-10 minutes. Thinner asparagus may cook faster.

Once the asparagus is removed from the air fryer, add a little more Parmesan cheese to finish it off! Enjoy immediately.

Fresh GREEN BEANS

READY IN 10 MIN   **SERVES 4**

Asian-inspired air fryer green beans are the perfect easy-to-make side dish that
you can enjoy all year long. Fresh green beans have never tasted so good!

DIRECTIONS

Preheat your air fryer to 400 degrees.

Place the trimmed green beans, sesame oil, garlic salt,
and pepper into a bowl and mix to evenly coat the
green beans.

Put the green beans into your preheated air fryer for 5-7
minutes, shaking the basket halfway through. You can
check the tenderness with a fork to test if the green
beans are done.

Remove green beans from the air fryer and enjoy!

INGREDIENTS

1 lb green beans, washed
and trimmed

2 tsp sesame oil

1 tsp garlic salt

pepper to taste

Tender CARROTS

READY IN **20 MIN**   SERVES **4**

INGREDIENTS

16 ounces of carrots

1 tsp oil

salt and pepper (to taste)

DIRECTIONS

Peel carrots and cut them into 2-inch chunks.
Cut any larger pieces in half to make all
pieces a similar size.

Preheat the air fryer to 360 degrees.

Toss carrots in about 1 teaspoon of oil. You
can omit the oil if you prefer, but it will result
in drier carrots.

Place the carrots in the air fryer and cook for
15-18 minutes, shaking every few minutes.

Test carrots with a fork for tenderness. They
are done when it glides through the carrot
easily.

Add salt and pepper to taste and shake the
basket to coat.

Serve and enjoy immediately.

FOR BABY CARROTS

If you prefer to use baby carrots, you can still
follow the same basic steps in this recipe.
Just up the air fryer temperature to 370
degrees, and cook for 12-15 minutes (until
tender).

Balsamic ROASTED VEGGIES

READY IN **20 MIN**   SERVES 2

INGREDIENTS

1 large zucchini,
sliced

2 red bell
peppers, roughly
chopped

10 cherry
tomatoes, halved

10 medium Bella
mushrooms, halved

3 small red onions,
peeled and halved

1 tsp olive oil

½ tsp salt

½ tsp freshly ground
pepper

½ tsp dried basil

½ tsp dried oregano

1 tbsp balsamic
vinegar, divided

DIRECTIONS

Preheat the air fryer to 390 F.

Place all the veggies in a large bowl. Add
the olive oil, salt, pepper, basil, oregano,
and ⅔ tablespoon balsamic vinegar. Stir well
until everything is coated.

Transfer the veggies to the air fryer basket,
arranging them in a single layer. Work in
batches. Air fry for 10 minutes, then repeat
for the remaining vegetables.

Drizzle the remaining balsamic vinegar over
the cooked veggies, as well as some extra
freshly ground pepper, if desired. Serve
warm.

The Best
CORN ON THE COB

READY IN **18 MIN**   SERVES **2**

Delicious corn on the cob is roasted to perfection and topped with parmesan cheese for a flavorful side dish.

INGREDIENTS

2 ears of corn

2 tbsp butter

½ tsp dried parsley (or 1 ½ tsp fresh)

¼ tsp sea salt

2 tbsp shredded parmesan cheese (or grated)

DIRECTIONS

Preheat your air fryer to 400 degrees. Meanwhile, shuck both ears of corn and remove any silk. Cut the corn in half if desired.

Mix together melted butter, parsley, and sea salt in a bowl. Baste on corn evenly. Wrap corn in foil if using (see tips section below for more information on this).

Place corn inside the air fryer side by side and cook for 12-14 minutes until some pieces are browned.

Remove the corn from the air fryer and roll in the parmesan cheese.

Enjoy immediately or place in the fridge for up to 3 days without cheese on top.

TIPS

While I love some roasting corn to the point it's browned in spots, I know it's not appealing for everyone. Air frying corn on the cob while wrapped in foil allows you to completely cook the corn while holding the flavor and finishes with bright yellow corn kernels.

To do this, first place the corn on a piece of aluminum foil and baste on the butter mixture. Next, fold the aluminum foil around the corn and cook according to this recipe. You can even cook them with your uncovered corn at the same time if you want to make both kinds (which we often do to please our picky eaters).

Caramelized BROCCOLI

READY IN **11 MIN**   SERVES **4**

Broccoli is air fried into a crispiness that can't be recreated anywhere else, then topped with fresh parmesan cheese to create an irresistable flavor combination.

DIRECTIONS

Preheat your air fryer to 400 degrees. Meanwhile, cut broccoli into florets and set aside.

Mix together melted butter, minced garlic, salt, pepper, and red pepper flakes (if using).

Add the broccoli and mix to combine thoroughly.

Add the parmesan cheese and mix again, making sure to coat it evenly.

Place broccoli into the air fryer and cook for 6-8 minutes, shaking the basket halfway through.*

Remove broccoli from the air fryer and serve immediately. Add additional parmesan cheese if desired.

*If broccoli is starting brown too much halfway through cooking, drop the temperature to 360 degrees and continue to cook according to the timing above.

INGREDIENTS

1 head of broccoli

2 tbsp butter, melted

1 clove garlic, minced

salt and pepper to taste

¼ cup parmesan cheese (freshly grated)

additional parmesan cheese for serving

pinch of red pepper flakes (optional)

Roasted MUSHROOMS

READY IN 18 MIN   **SERVES 2**

INGREDIENTS

10 oz mushrooms,
sliced

1 tbsp olive oil

2 garlic cloves,
minced

½ tsp salt

½ tsp freshly ground
pepper

⅓ cup parmesan,
grated, divided

1 tbsp fresh parsley,
chopped

DIRECTIONS

Preheat the air fryer to 360F.

In a large bowl, add the mushrooms, oil,
garlic, salt, pepper, and half of the
parmesan.

Transfer the mushroom slices to the air fryer
basket.

Roast for 7-8 minutes, stirring once.

Top with the remaining parmesan and fresh
parsley to serve.

Portobello MUSHROOMS

READY IN **22 MIN**　　　SERVES **3-4**

Even mushroom skeptics will come around once they try a bite of an air fryer portobello mushroom! This easy vegan and keto recipe is ready in just over 20 minutes.

DIRECTIONS

Preheat your air fryer to 350 degrees.

Remove the stem from your mushroom cap by carefully pulling the cap to the side so it pops out.

Hold your mushroom cap under slowly running water and gently rub it to remove any dirt from the outside and inside of the cap. Pat them dry with paper towels.

Zest your lemon with a zester or grater. Then cut your lemon in half to juice it. Wash your herbs and pat them dry.

In a small food processor or blender, place your herbs, garlic, lemon zest and juice, and olive oil. Blend until smooth. Using a basting brush, brush the mushrooms on the top and bottom till they are covered.

Place the mushroom caps top side down and cook at 350 degrees F for 10 minutes. Then flip the caps for an additional 2 minutes.

INGREDIENTS

3 to 4 portobello mushroom caps

Juice and zest of 1 lemon

¼ cup parsley, loosely packed

¼ cup oregano, loosely packed

2 tbsp loosely packed thyme

1 tbsp garlic, minced

3 tbsp olive oil, divided

Fried OKRA

READY IN **17 MIN**   SERVES **4**

INGREDIENTS

12 ounces okra, cut into 1/2-inch slices with tops and bottoms removed

½ cup flour

2 eggs

⅓ cup cornmeal

⅓ cup breadcrumbs

½ teaspoon paprika

sea salt or table salt, to taste

Pinch of cayenne pepper (optional)

DIRECTIONS

Preheat your air fryer to 380 degrees.

Set out 2 medium bowls and 1 small bowl. Fill a medium bowl with flour, the small bowl with the eggs, and the remaining medium bowl with the cornmeal, breadcrumbs, paprika, and cayenne pepper (if using).

Take turns dipping each piece of okra into the flour mixture, then the eggs, then the cornmeal mixture coating it on all sides each time.

Place the breaded okra in the air fryer and spritz them with a little oil, then cook for 7 to 8 minutes until golden brown on the outside.

Remove the okra from the air fryer enjoy!

TIP

When dredging the okra in the flour, eggs, and cornmeal, I use a fork to pick up each piece of okra, which makes it a lot easier!

Roasted RADISHES

READY IN **15 MIN**   SERVES **4**

INGREDIENTS

1 bunch of radishes, washed, trimmed, and quartered (about 12-15 radishes)

2 tbsp olive oil

½ tsp garlic powder

½ tsp salt

¼ tsp black pepper

Fresh parsley for garnish (optional)

DIRECTIONS

Preheat the air fryer to 400 F

In a medium bowl, toss the chopped radishes with olive oil and seasonings until everything is uniformly mixed

Add the radishes to the air fryer in a single layer and cook for 8-10 minutes, shaking the basket at the halfway mark, or until tender on the inside

TIPS

If you've never tried roasted radishes before, you might wonder what they taste like, and what to do with them. This recipe makes a mild-flavored radish that has a light seasoning. I often substitute them for potato wedges when I want a lower carb option!

DELICIOUS
Air Fryer
DESSERTS

Moist
CHOCOLATE CAKE
READY IN **55 MIN**   SERVES **6-8**

INGREDIENTS

1 cup granulated sugar

¾ cup plus 2 tablespoons all-purpose flour

½ cup unsweetened cocoa powder

1 tsp baking powder

½ tsp baking soda

½ tsp kosher salt

1 large egg

½ cup buttermilk

¼ cup vegetable oil

1 tsp vanilla extract

½ cup boiling water

Use simple, everyday ingredients to whip up a rich and decadent chocolate cake in your air fryer! This recipe gives you that deep chocolate flavor while being light and fluffy.

DIRECTIONS

Preheat your air fryer to 350°F and spray the inside of a 7-in. cake pan with baking spray. Line with a 9-inch round piece of parchment paper.

In a large bowl, whisk together the sugar, flour, cocoa powder, baking powder, baking soda, and salt. Add the egg, buttermilk, vegetable oil, and vanilla extract.

Mix for 2 minutes and then stir in the boiling water to create a thin batter.

Pour the batter into the pan and place it in the air fryer basket.

Cook for 25 minutes or until the cake is baked through.

Cool in the pan for 10 minutes, then remove to a wire rack to cool completely.

Decorate with frosting and sprinkles!

TIPS

Want to store it for later? These tips will help!

If the cake is unfrosted, wrap it in plastic wrap. Store at room temperature for two days or in the refrigerator for up to a week.

If the cake is frosted, cover it loosely with plastic wrap or foil, so you don't smear the frosting. Store in the refrigerator and enjoy within a week.

Nutella
LAVA CAKES

READY IN **20 MIN**   SERVES **2**

INGREDIENTS

½ cup semi-sweet chocolate chips

4 tbsp butter

½ cup powdered sugar

3 tbsp all-purpose flour

2 eggs

1 tsp vanilla extract

¼ tsp salt

NUTELLA FILLING

2 tbsp Nutella

1 tbsp butter (softened)

1 tbsp powdered sugar

Filled with warm, gooey, hazelnut-and-chocolate lava, these air fryer lava cakes are great desserts for any occasion!

DIRECTIONS

Preheat your air fryer to 370°F.

In a medium microwave-safe bowl, add the chocolate chips and butter and heat in 30-second intervals until completely melted, stirring during each interval.

Add the powdered sugar, flour, eggs, vanilla, and salt to the bowl and whisk to combine.

In a separate bowl, mix the Nutella, softened butter, and powdered sugar.

Prepare the ramekins by spraying them with oil and fill each one-half full with the chocolate mixture.

Add half of the Nutella filling in the center of each ramekin, then top off with the remaining chocolate mixture.

Place the lava cakes into the air fryer and cook for 8 to 11 minutes.

Carefully remove the lava cakes and allow them to cool for 5 minutes.

Take a butterknife and run around the outside edges of the cake and flip it out onto a serving plate.

Top with ice cream and chocolate syrup. Enjoy!

INGREDIENTS

1 stick butter (softened)

½ cup + 2 tbsp brown sugar (packed)

¼ cup sugar

1 egg

1 tsp vanilla extract

1 ½ cups all-purpose flour

½ tsp baking soda

½ tsp salt

1 cup semi-sweet chocolate chips

Chocolate
COOKIE CAKE

READY IN **25 MIN**   SERVES **2**

Want to quickly whip up a batch of warm chocolate chip cookies? Bake them in the air fryer. These cookies turn out perfectly, and they come out soft and chewy on the inside with a slightly crisp edge.

DIRECTIONS

Preheat the air fryer to 370°F.

In a large bowl, mix the butter, brown sugar, and sugar until creamy.

Add the vanilla and eggs and mix until thoroughly combined. Slowly add in the flour, baking soda, and salt until just mixed.

Then, stir in the chocolate chips to just combine them with the batter.

Spray a 6-inch pan with oil, then add half of the batter into the pan and compress the batter to evenly fill the pan.

Save the other half in the fridge or freezer for later.

Place the cookie in the air fryer and cook for 10 minutes.

Remove it from the air fryer and let it cool for about 5 minutes.

Remove the cookie from the pan, and top it with some vanilla ice cream and your favorite toppings.

Enjoy!

Chocolate Chip COOKIES

READY IN **35 MIN**   SERVES **4**

DIRECTIONS

In a mixing bowl, combine softened butter and sugar.

Then, add salt, eggs, and vanilla extract. Mix well!

Add the flour, cocoa powder, and baking powder, and mix until everything is combined. Stir in the chocolate chips and walnuts (if using) until just combined.

Place a piece of parchment paper in the air fryer basket.

Make small balls from the dough, and arrange them on the parchment with enough space between them.

Bake the cookies for 15- 20 minutes at 300°F.

When cookies are golden brown, let them stay in the air fryer basket for an additional 1 to 2 minutes.

Serve with a glass of milk, and enjoy!

INGREDIENTS

½ cup softened butter (unsalted)

½ cup sugar

2 eggs

½ tsp vanilla extract

pinch of salt

1 ⅓ cups all-purpose flour

3 tsp cocoa powder

½ tsp baking powder

½ cup chocolate chips

½ cup walnuts (optional)

Easy
FRIED OREOS

READY IN **10 MIN**   SERVES **8**

INGREDIENTS

8 Oreo cookies

1 package of Pillsbury crescents rolls

powdered sugar for dusting (optional)

Think fluffy, creamy, and chocolatey... That's what these "deep-fried" Oreos taste like. But without all the grease. So go ahead and indulge. I won't tell!

DIRECTIONS

Spread out crescent dough onto a cutting board or counter.

Using your finger, press down on each perforated line so it forms one big sheet.

Cut the dough into eighths.

Place an Oreo cookie in the center of each of the crescent roll squares and roll each corner up.

Bunch up the rest of the crescent roll to make sure it covers the entire Oreo cookie.

Preheat the air fryer to 320°F for about 2-3 minutes.

Gently place Oreos inside the air fryer in one even row, so they do not touch.

Bake for 5-6 minutes until golden brown on the outside.

Carefully remove "fried" Oreos from the air fryer and immediately dust them with powdered sugar.

Let cool for two minutes, then enjoy!

Fudgy BROWNIES

READY IN **20 MIN**   SERVES **4**

INGREDIENTS

½ cup all-purpose flour

½ cup sugar

½ cup cocoa powder

½ tsp baking powder

½ cup dark chocolate (melted)

3 tbsp butter

3 large eggs

1 tbsp extra virgin olive oil

½ tsp vanilla extract

pinch of salt

DIRECTIONS

In a mixing bowl, combine the flour, sugar, cocoa powder, and baking powder.

Melt the butter and chocolate, then whisk in the eggs. Add in the olive oil, vanilla, and a pinch of salt.

Add the dry ingredients to the wet ingredients, and mix until everything is combined.

Prepare the baking pan by spraying it with oil or using a piece of parchment paper.

Bake 300°F for 20 minutes in the air fryer. To have more fudge texture, the middle must be soft.

Let it stay in the air fryer basket for an additional 1 to 2 minutes.

Slice and enjoy!

Glazed DONUTS

READY IN 17 MIN   **SERVES 8**

It's so easy to make air fryer donuts with Pillsbury grand biscuit dough! The
3-ingredient glaze is the perfect icing on top for homemade donuts.
Great for a fun breakfast with the kids.

DIRECTIONS

Preheat air fryer to 350 degrees.

Using a small circular cookie cutter about 1-2 inches in
diameter, cut a hole into the middle of the doughnut.

Place doughnuts and donut holes into air fryer in one
single layer and cook for 4-5 minutes until golden brown
and cooked thoroughly.

Meanwhile, put the easy glaze together by whisking the 3
ingredients together. Add the extra tablespoon of milk if
needed for better consistency.

Carefully remove the donuts from the air fryer and
immediately dip them into the glaze.

Place on a wire rack to cool for at least 2 minutes, then
enjoy!

INGREDIENTS

1 package Pillsbury
Grand Rolls (flaky or
homestyle)

GLAZE

2 cups confectioner's
sugar

1 tsp vanilla extract

2-3 tbsp milk

INGREDIENTS

1 package Pillsbury Grands (homestyle)

1 tbsp butter (melted)

½ cup sugar

½ cup seedless raspberry jelly

Sugary
JELLY DONUTS

READY IN 15 **MIN**   SERVES **8**

Having a major sweet tooth this morning? These raspberry jelly-filled donuts are the perfect treat! They're easy to make and only require 4 simple ingredients.

DIRECTIONS

Preheat the air fryer to 320°F.

Place grand rolls inside the air fryer in a single layer and cook for 5-6 minutes until golden brown.

Remove rolls from the air fryer and set aside.

Place sugar into a wide bowl with a flat bottom.

Baste the melted butter on all sides of the donut and roll in the sugar to cover completely.

Repeat with all of the remaining donuts.

Using a long cake tip, pipe 1-2 tablespoons of raspberry jelly into each donut.

Enjoy!

TIPS

Donuts are best when eaten warm!

If not consumed immediately, you can store the rolls after cooked for up to 3 days. When ready to eat, reheat in a preheated air fryer at 300°F for 2-3 minutes, then coat with butter and sugar and pipe jelly in when ready to eat.

Not a fan of raspberry jelly? Swap it out for your favorite! I recommend strawberry, mixed berry, and grape jelly.

Cinnamon APPLE WEDGES

READY IN 15 MIN   **SERVES 6**

INGREDIENTS

3 Granny Smith
apples

1 cup flour

3 eggs (whisked)

1 cup graham
cracker crumbs

¼ cup sugar

1 tsp ground
cinnamon

DIRECTIONS

Preheat your air fryer to 380°F.

Cut the apples into wedges and remove the
core.

Using 3 bowls, place the flour in the first
bowl, the egg in the second bowl, and mix
the graham cracker crumbs, sugar, and
cinnamon in the third bowl.

Dip an apple wedge into the flour, then the
egg, and lastly, the graham cracker mixture.
Making sure to coat the apple as best as
possible each time.

Repeat with remaining apple slices.

Place apples into the air fryer in one layer
spaced on and cook for 5-6 minutes, flipping
them with one minute left.

Remove the apples from the air fryer.

Serve with caramel sauce, and enjoy!

Baked APPLES

READY IN 20 MIN   **SERVES 4**

INGREDIENTS

4 large apples
3 tbsp quick oats

2 tbsp golden
raisins

2 tbsp chopped
pecans

2 tbsp light brown
sugar

2 tbsp melted
unsalted butter

1/2 tsp apple pie
seasoning

DIRECTIONS

Cut the tops of your apples off and then
slightly cut the bottom of your apple off so
that it is flat on the bottom.

Using a paring knife, remove the center of the
apple (don't go all the way), about an inch
wide.

In a medium bowl, combine the oats, raisins,
pecans, brown sugar, melted butter, and
apple pie seasoning.

Divide the mixture among the 4 apples, filling
in the centers.

Place your apples in the air fryer and bake at
300°F for 13-15 minutes until they are
perfectly soft.

Allow them to sit for a few minutes, as they
will be very hot to remove.

Once you have removed them, serve warm
and for an additional treat, top with a dollop
of vanilla ice cream.

Enjoy!

Apple
PIE ROLLS

READY IN **30 MIN**   SERVES **4**

INGREDIENTS

1 cup canned apple pie
filling (or homemade)

8 egg roll wrappers

1 tbsp butter melted
(unsalted or salted will work)

1 tsp ground cinnamon

Apple pie rolls are an easy way to enjoy your favorite fall
dessert! These air-fried pie rolls are perfect for a quick snack
or a fun treat!

DIRECTIONS

Preheat the air fryer to 400°F.

Lay the egg roll wrapper on a flat surface, with the tip of the
triangle facing you (like a diamond).

Place a scoop of apple filling on the edge of the wrapper
(below the center).

Fold the bottom corner over the filling, and moisten the
remaining wrapper edges with water.

Fold side corners toward the center over filling.

Roll the egg roll up tightly, pressing at the tip to seal.

Repeat with the rest.

Place parchment paper in the fryer basket.

Arrange egg rolls in a single layer.

Use a culinary brush to grease rolls with butter and sprinkle
some cinnamon on top.

Cook until golden brown, about 10-12 minutes.

Serve and enjoy!

Crispy APPLE CHIPS

READY IN **14 MIN**   SERVES **1**

DIRECTIONS

Wash and dry your apple. Cut into 1/8-inch slices with a knife or mandolin.

Lay your apple slices into your air fryer basket. Sprinkle with cinnamon.

Set the temperature to 360°F and air fry for 8-12 minutes, flipping at the 5-minute mark. The smaller slices may come out before the larger slices.

Once they are done cooking, let them sit in the basket for 5 minutes. This will help them crisp up more.

TIPS

There are many options of apples you could use for this recipe, such as Pink Lady, Golden Delicious, or Fuji. Find your favorite by trying out a few different types! Once you've made the perfect apple chips, keep any leftovers in an airtight container so they'll stay fresh longer.

INGREDIENTS

1 Gala apple

1-1 ½ tsp of cinnamon

Cinnamon Sugar DESSERT FRIES

READY IN **20 MIN**   SERVES **4**

DIRECTIONS

Preheat your air fryer to 380°F.

Peel and cut the sweet potatoes into skinny fries.

Coat fries with 1 tablespoon of butter.

Cook fries in the preheated air fryer for 15-18 minutes. (They can overlap, but should not fill your air fryer more than 1/2 full)

Remove the sweet potato fries from the air fryer and place them in a bowl.

Coat with the remaining butter and add in sugar and cinnamon.

Mix to coat.

Enjoy immediately!

INGREDIENTS

2 sweet potatoes

1 tbsp butter (melted)

1 tsp butter (melted and separated from the above)

2 tbsp sugar

1/2 tsp cinnamon

Pumpkin PIE TWISTS

READY IN **13 MIN**   SERVES **8**

DIRECTIONS

Roll out crescent roll dough and press down on any perforated lines.

Cut dough into quarters by making one cut length-wise and then again width-wise.

Add pumpkin puree, half of the pumpkin pie spice, and salt, then mix to combine.

Spread the pumpkin puree on top of the dough.

Place 2 dough sheets on top of the other two, pumpkin side down.

Using a pizza cutter, cut each pumpkin twist sheet into 4 long strips, making a total of 8.

Preheat air fryer to 320°F for 2-3 minutes.

Twist each strip 1-2 times on the bottom and 1-2 times on the top.

Brush melted butter on top of the pumpkin pie twists and sprinkle with remaining pumpkin pie spice.

Place the pumpkin twists into the air fryer evenly in one layer and not touching. Cook for 6 minutes.

Meanwhile, make the icing by whisking the confectionery sugar, melted butter, and milk in a bowl.

Remove twists from the air fryer and drizzle with icing.

Enjoy immediately or store in a refrigerator for up to 3 days!

INGREDIENTS

1 can Pillsbury crescent rolls

½ cup pumpkin puree

2 tsp pumpkin pie spice

⅛ tsp salt

3 tbsp unsalted butter (melted)

ICING

½ cup confectionery sugar

2 tbsp melted butter

2 and ¼ tsp milk

Sweet CHERRY CRUMBLE

READY IN 40 MIN   **SERVES 4**

INGREDIENTS

1 cup canned cherry filling (or home-made)

½ cup softened butter (unsalted)

½ cup brown sugar

pinch of salt

½ tsp baking powder

1 egg yolk

2 tbsp rolled oats (optional)

1 cup flour

DIRECTIONS

In the mixing bowl, combine softened butter and sugar. Mix well.

Add salt, egg yolk, oats, baking powder, and flour.

Combine everything (the dough must be tough).

Prepare the baking dish and spray some oil on it.

Take half of the dough and crush it with your fingers.

Add the crumble to the baking dish, and then add the cherry filling.

On top of it, add the second half of the dough.

Bake the crumble for 20-25 minutes at 300°F in the air fryer.

When the crumble is golden brown, let it stay in the air fryer basket for an additional 5 minutes.

Serve with a scoop of ice cream, and enjoy!

Caramelized PEACH BOWLS

READY IN **15 MIN**   SERVES **2**

DIRECTIONS

Rinse fresh peaches, pat dry with towels, and slice them in half.

Remove pits from the middle.

Brush the coconut oil on both sides of the peaches.

Place peaches in a single layer in your air fryer basket, and sprinkle with brown sugar and cinnamon.

Bake at 350°F for 5-10 minutes.

Place peaches onto the plate, and serve with a scoop of vanilla ice cream.

Enjoy!

INGREDIENTS

2 fresh peaches

1 tsp coconut oil

1 tbsp brown sugar

½ tsp ground cinnamon (optional)

1 cup vanilla ice cream

Sweet CARAMELIZED BANANAS

READY IN **17 MIN**   SERVES **2-3**

DIRECTIONS

Preheat the air fryer to 400°F.

Mix the sugar and cinnamon in a bowl.

Coat all the banana slices with this mixture.

Prep the air fryer basket with parchment paper and arrange the banana slices in the basket in a single layer.

Air fry for 5 minutes to get firm caramelized bananas or 7 minutes if you prefer them softer.

Serve with a teaspoon of whipped cream, and enjoy!

TIPS

These air-fried caramelized bananas taste delicious on their own but you can also serve them with some pancakes and waffles or serve them over some ice cream.

INGREDIENTS

2 bananas (cut into slices)

4 tbsp brown sugar

½ tsp cinnamon

2 tsp whipped cream (optional)

Gooey S'MORES

READY IN **4 MIN**   SERVES **4**

This air fryer s'mores recipe is the perfect dessert with crispy, golden-brown marshmallows topped off with a piece of chocolate and graham crackers for a delicious treat!

DIRECTIONS

Preheat the air fryer to 380°F.

Place graham crackers in the air fryer and top with marshmallows.

Place a wire rack on top of the marshmallows to avoid them from flying up in the air fryer.

Cook for 3 to 4 minutes until the marshmallow is golden brown.

Remove s'mores from the air fryer, add 3 chocolate bar squares to each s'more, and top with the other graham cracker.

Enjoy!

INGREDIENTS

12 squares from a Hershey's chocolate bar (1 regular-sized Hershey bar)

4 marshmallows (big or jumbo-sized)

4 graham crackers sheets (broken in half)

Cinnamon Sugar CHURROS

READY IN **30 MIN**   SERVES **4**

DIRECTIONS

In a medium saucepan, add water, butter, sugar, and salt.

Bring to a boil, add flour into the boiling mixture, stirring constantly until the dough becomes soft and smooth, about 3-5 minutes.

Let the dough cool down a bit, add eggs, and mix well. Transfer the dough to a pastry bag fitted with a star-shaped tip.

Place parchment paper in the air fryer basket and spray with oil. Pipe churros on it and spray coconut oil.

Bake at 370°F for 10-15 minutes until golden brown.

Combine sugar and cinnamon in a bowl.

Once churros are ready, transfer them to the bowl with sugar and toss to coat.

Serve with chocolate or caramel sauce, and enjoy!

INGREDIENTS

⅔ cup water

½ cup butter

1 tbsp sugar

pinch of salt

½ cup flour

sugar and cinnamon (for coating)

1 tbsp coconut oil

2 large eggs

Chocolate
BREAD PUDDING

READY IN **25 MIN**   SERVES **2**

INGREDIENTS

1 large egg

3-4 slices of white bread

½ cup whole milk

¼ cup heavy cream
(optional)

2 tbsp white sugar (or brown
sugar)

2 tbsp walnuts (chopped)

2 tbsp dark chocolate
(chopped or chocolate
chips)

½ tsp vanilla extract

¼ tsp orange peels

Pinch of cinnamon (optional)

This chocolate and orange bread pudding is the delicious dessert you've been waiting for! It's easy to make and can be tailored to your own taste. Serve it hot or cold, with or without whipped cream- the choice is yours! And best of all, it can be made in your air fryer.

DIRECTIONS

Preheat the air fryer to 330°F.

Break the bread into small pieces or cut it into small squares with a knife.

Grease your cake pan and place the bread in it.

Crack the egg into a separate bowl and whisk.

Add milk, heavy cream (if using), sugar, vanilla extract, and cinnamon.

Pour the egg mixture into the pan with the bread and mix with a spoon.

Add chopped nuts, chocolate, and orange peel.

Place the baking pan inside the air fryer basket and bake for about 15 minutes until the top is golden brown.

TIPS

If you don't want to use chopped chocolate, swap it out for some chocolate chips instead!

THANK YOU

I hope you've enjoyed this cookbook and that these recipes have brought joy to you and your family. If you have any suggestions or feedback, just drop me a note at Samantha@everydayfamilycooking.com. I love hearing from my readers!

In the meantime, enjoy cooking and feasting with your loved ones.

Printed in Great Britain
by Amazon

48527881R00106